Larry Larsen's Guide to

North Florida Bass Waters

by Larry Larsen

Book I in the Bass Waters Series

A LARSEN'S OUTDOOR PUBLISHING BOOK
THE ROWMAN & LITTLEFIELD PUBLISHING GROUP, INC.
Lanham • Chicago • New York • Toronto • Plymouth, UK

Published by
LARSEN'S OUTDOOR PUBLISHING
An imprint of The Rowman & Littlefield Publishing Group, Inc.
4501 Forbes Boulevard, Suite 200, Lanham, Maryland 20706
http://www.rlpgtrade.com

Estover Road, Plymouth PL6 7PY, United Kingdom

Distributed by National Book Network

British Library Cataloguing in Publication Information Available

Library of Congress Cataloging-in-Publication Data Available

Library of Congress 91-76436

ISBN: 978-0-936513-15-7 (paper : alk.paper)

♾™ The paper used in this publication meets the minimum
requirements of American National Standard for Information
Sciences—Permanence of Paper for Printed Library Materials,
ANSI/NISO Z39.48-1992.

Printed in the United States of America

ACKNOWLEDGMENTS

I want to thank the guides of North Florida that I have fished with over the past 24 years. Their sharing of knowledge regarding the region's lakes and rivers have helped in this effort. I also am grateful to Bob Knops of Fishing Hot Spots for his assistance in developing individual lake maps sprinkled throughout this series of books. Thanks also to my friends in the Jacksonville bass clubs, in the Florida Outdoor Writers Association and others who shared a boat with me on most of the waters mentioned in this book.

Thanks go to Frank Sargeant, Rick Farren, Shaw Grigsby, Dan Thurmond, Terry LaCoss, Jack Wingate and Johnny Pate. Thanks also to my friends in the media, those newspaper and magazine columnists and editors who are interested in sharing with their readers information about my entire line of outdoor books. I appreciate their kind comments.

Special thanks go to my wife, Lilliam. Her valuable contribution in reviewing, design layout and production assistance to develop "Larry Larsen's Guide To North Florida Bass Waters" is much appreciated.

3

PREFACE

If you want to learn more about your favorite water, or learn about other overlooked hotspots in this region, this Guide is for you.

If your favorite water is not mentioned, there could be several reasons:

1. The author is not aware of the productivity of your favorite spot;
2. With so many waters to cover, it is impossible to mention each and every one;
3. The author may just be keeping it a secret for himself!

This book should be a reference source for all anglers who fish or wish to fish in the future the waters of North Florida. Each chapter focuses on the "name" lakes in the region that almost always produce good bass fishing and on many overlooked waters that quietly produce good bass fishing as well. The places mentioned in each chapter are waters where you can usually catch largemouth bass.

Those waters where sunshine (hybrid striped bass), striped bass, spotted bass, shoal bass, redeye bass and Suwannee bass are also noted on occasion. Also, the book reveals the waters where the smaller species of sunfish "think they are bass." Some of these bullies may even out-fight a bass!

Additionally, productive methods that will help the reader catch more and larger bass on these waters are presented in **Larry Larsen's Guide To North Florida Bass Waters.** The proven techniques, lures and baits discussed within the pages of this book should help you be better prepared to tackle one of the rivers or lakes in the book on your next time out.

CONTENTS

The author has extensively covered the region's bass waters to research magazine articles and books. He has caught several hundred bass from 5 to 12 pounds from Florida lakes and rivers.

INTRODUCTION

THE GUIDE AND YOUR GUIDE

Learn everything there is to know about your next North Florida bass fishing destination and your trip will be better planned and more productive. **Guide To North Florida Bass Waters** is your best resource for trip planning, seasonal information, water characteristics and other interesting and necessary details that will make your bass fishing trip less of a guessing game.

You may be surprised to learn that many of the Florida state records, and even several world record fish come from North Florida. Many are of the black bass family, such as the redeye, Suwannee, spotted and shoal bass. **Guide To North Florida Bass Waters** focuses on the top bass rivers and lakes from the western tip of the Florida Panhandle east to the Atlantic Ocean and south to, and including St. Johns, Clay, Alachua and Levy Counties. This region is the most productive in terms of big fish for all bass species!

To help you better locate productive spots, the book lists specific locations on each of the waters covered, and techniques that the author and other expert bass guides and professional fishermen have employed to more effectively fish them. Launching areas, maps and other lake details are also included for many of the region's lakes and rivers.

While largemouth bass is the main focus of this book, many other bass species are also mentioned. Many of these waters are home to more than largemouth bass and should provide anglers with a varied challenge. Suwannee bass, spotted bass, redeye and shoal bass are profiled in their favorite North Florida habitat. So are striped bass, hybrid striped bass (sunshine bass) and white bass. Information on lake records is included, for those anglers wishing to prepare in advance to try to set their own.

The specific waters within these pages were picked because they are consistently productive for numbers or bass, and/or because they produce lunker-size largemouth or other bass species. These waters are also popular, with a local reputation for quality fisheries, and are accessible to most anglers with canoes, johnboats or larger bass boats. If your favorite lake or river isn't mentioned, it may be because it's too small and heavy fishing pressure could devastate it, or because it's private, or because it's currently not known to be productive. Finally, it may simply be located in a different region, so check the other books in this series.

Some of the most interesting and valuable aspects of **Guide to North Florida Bass Waters** are the seasonal information, lures and tackle recommendations, and detailed locations mentioned for improving the angler's bass catching success. The author, Larry Larsen, takes the time to outline specific locations in lakes, rivers and creeks, information that is normally not possible to include in many magazine articles due to lack of space. It is certain that the reader will learn much new information revealed in this book for the first time.

Larry quickly learned how productive North Florida bass waters could be. On his very first day in Florida, Larry and a visitor from Alabama caught 7 bass that weighed 68 pounds in just one hour's time.

In the 24 years since then, Larry has covered the state in his quest for great bass waters...from the sand hill ponds in Holmes and Walton Counties to Titusville's Merritt Island Refuge, from the St. Mary's River at the Georgia line to the brackish canals in the Everglades. Fishing more than 1,000 of Florida's lakes and rivers qualify him to author the Guide to Florida Bass Waters series of books.

It is improbable at least that readers would not learn something from Larry's knowledge and experience. An award-winning author of nine other books on bass fishing, few writers are more qualified and knowledgeable about Florida's bass waters. He enjoys Florida bass fishing as much as he enjoys writing about it, and he's as good an angler as he is a writer.

His Florida fishing success includes numerous bass between five and 12 pounds from the waters mentioned. He also held a line-class world record for Suwannee bass. His expertise in developing successful patterns for both artificial and live bait fishing has resulted in extensive recording of his catches and successes through several thousand color slides and magazine articles.

Over the past eight years, Larry has covered the state for Outdoor Life as their Florida Editor, fishing and writing about the top waters and those often overlooked. His numerous articles on Florida bass waters have also appeared in Florida Sportsman, and many other regional and national publications. He is a member of the Outdoor Writers Association of America (OWAA), the Southeastern Outdoor Press Association (SEOPA), and the Florida Outdoor Writers Association (FOWA).

The **Guide to North Florida Bass Waters** is the first of the Bass Waters Series, which includes Central Florida and South Florida Bass Waters.

Guide to North Florida Bass Waters includes several appendices that an informed reader should find of interest. Appendix A lists the significant lakes and rivers in each North Florida county and the surface acreage of each. The addresses and telephone numbers of the responsible game and fish office and those of the county chambers of commerce are listed in Appendix B.

To help broaden your knowledge on bass fishing, inshore fishing and hunting for deer and turkey, Appendix C is the informative Fishing & Hunting Resource Directory. A compilation of quality outdoor reference books that are extremely popular with sportsmen is presented. For example, Larry's award-winning 9-book BASS SERIES LIBRARY details highly productive fish catching methods and special techniques. Other books published by Larsen's Outdoor Publishing reveal how to be more productive on your next fishing or hunting trip. This additional information in the Resource Directory will help you catch more bass and inshore fish, and locate more deer and turkey on your next hunting. They will help make you more successful!

Information on how to obtain the most comprehensive maps for many of the state's lakes is also available in Appendix D.

Finally, the comprehensive Index includes a cross reference of lakes, cities, bass species, counties and fisheries information that will help you quickly locate and review each reference throughout the book.

I'm sure you will enjoy learning from Larry's expertise, as I have over the years. -- Lilliam M. Larsen

1

ORANGE LAKE - LUNKERS IN LOW LIGHT

THE ULTRA-QUIET period of a summer evening can make the most boat-shy bass forget the daylight congestion on Orange Lake. Bass in the heavily-fished lake become less cautious and move shallower to feed when the sun goes down. Night angling on this lake offers a unique experience and usually several thrills.

My line, as well as the eyes of several alligators, were illuminated only by the lunar rays, but I felt the rod twitch. I set the hook and scanned the surface for the healthy largemouth making a commotion on top, some 40 feet away.

The two-pound Orange Lake largemouth leaped moonward twice more before I could really enjoy the action visually. As it neared the boat, a large splash to my right temporarily distracted me. It was either one of the alligators or a record bass spooking. I chose to believe it was the latter.

Surviving droughts and vegetation plagues, the lake has remained one of the state's top bass waters!

I brought the fish aboard, turned on my dim night light and carefully extracted the hook. The fish, my twelfth bass, was also quickly released. Despite the action over the previous four hours, I was drowsy, so this tired and happy angler called it a night.

Lakes like Orange, that heat up during the day and cool down nicely at night, are prime candidates for good after-dark angling. The cooler temperatures at night keep the hordes of fishermen off the water. Usually, the relatively clear waters offer better fishing at night than during the day.

The most productive waters after dark are generally the busiest during the daylight. Heavy daytime boating/fishing pressure on

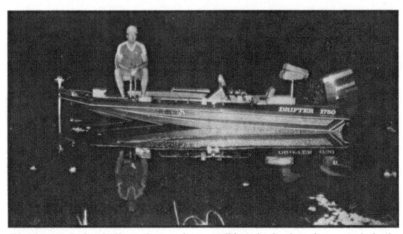

The Orange Lake shallows that produce small bass in the day often contain lunker bass in the low light.

Orange Lake continually disturbs the best accessible fishing areas and creates night feeding patterns. After the boaters have departed, bass become less wary and are overcome by their hunger.

Naturally, for best results, only those waters with which you are complete familiar should be fished at night. Orange is an easy lake to fish. As the last natural light begins to fade, look around for landmarks in relation to distant lights. Under a full moon you can see the shoreline, but on a new moon you are virtually blind without landmarks or artificial light of some sort.

The 'harvest' moon in its full power puts out enough light to cast shadows over Orange. Logs, cypress trees and vegetation will be reflected as a dark shadow on the bottom in shallow water. In deeper waters, the water column directly behind the moon ray interruption (for example, a floating clump of aquatic plants) will be darkened. In that spot, behind or beneath the cover, a bass can often be found waiting for a hapless prey to swim or crawl by within 'pouncing' distance. Frogs, freshwater eels, waterdogs and small bullhead catfish are usually more active at night.

Fortunately, for most anglers, largemouth are less dependent on good structure during moonless evenings. Transmitter studies by fisheries biologists on Orange have proven that bass will move around more at night than during daylight hours. They can totally utilize an extremely shallow area at night, whereas they may confine themselves to deeper, vegetated points during the day.

14

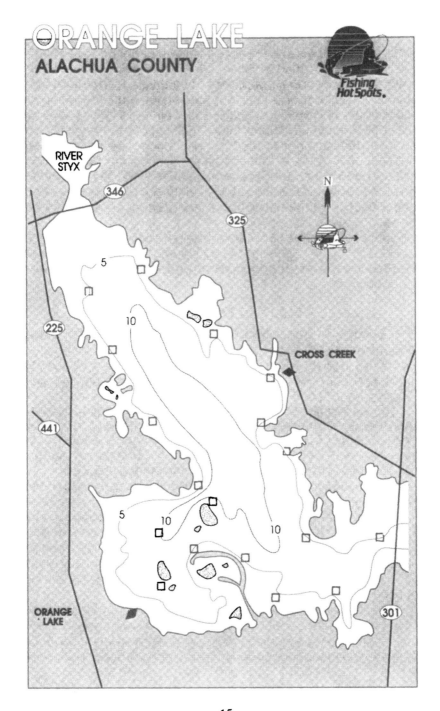

ORANGE LAKE

ALACHUA COUNTY

RIVER STYX

346

325

N

5

10

225

CROSS CREEK

441

5

10

10

ORANGE LAKE

301

Orange Lake's midnight-feeding bass prefer still water and are often found in the shallows near a deep water drop off. Productive fishermen fish off the bottom on moonlit nights or around light-colored areas so their lures are silhouetted against the 'light' source. Bass hiding in the shadows of structure will move along the shaded sides of cover. As night sets in, better fish movement may take place along the sides of long bars that exist in the lake.

Just after a rain shower is a great time to be on darkened Orange Lake waters. Cloudy nights during a full moon phase usually result in optimal pH levels and some fantastic bass catches in the shallows. Daytime pH values during a drought may be inordinately high in thin waters. Runoffs after a storm are a real find.

Some pretty large bass have been taken at night from Orange Lake, such as the lake record of 17 pounds, 4 ounces. The huge bass struck a black Jitterbug and took off, only to be subdued after a brief battle.

TACTICS, LURES & BAITS

Lures like a Jitterbug or Jerkin' Sam are favorites of successful moonlight anglers seeking trophy bass. The slow and steady retrieve offers an attractive gurgling noise to feeding predators. Bass are drawn to the 'disturbance' from several yards away, and then focus on the movement.

Buzzbaits do well in darkness, particularly when there is a slight wind-ripple on the surface. On very still nights, lure tossers often choose a noisy, weedless spoon for areas around dense vegetation. Again, plastic worms with a tail that does something: swim, vibrate, flap, flutter, etc., are extremely productive.

Night action on Orange Lake largemouth can be exceptional, but the good fishing is not limited only to dark hours. In the daytime, shallow top waters baits fished over hydrilla are bound to attract bass. The best hydrilla spots are those whose tops are barely under the water surface. Don't ignore the small islands of heavily matted hydrilla. In the summer, the best cover is usually located in the deepest water available offering protection and shade.

Fishermen who have already battled with one of the lakes' lunkers normally use 17 to 20 pound line test and baitcasting reels. Shiner fishermen usually cast 20 to 30 pound test monofilament on these vegetated waters, and shiners are very effective in the cooler

Texas-rigged scented worms account for many of Orange Lake's daylight largemouth. Flippers use a quiet approach to score.

spring and fall months. One of the better early spring techniques is to run upwind to a lee shore and drift downwind working the deeper areas just off the vegetation.

Flippin' a 7-inch worm in crawdad or pumpkinseed color is considered perhaps the best technique at Orange Lake. Black with blue tail plastic worms, and black grape, have also been proven fish catchers. Flippin' the islands or vegetation clumps in the summer is also productive. When tossing a worm, though, be prepared to haul in as much hydrilla as bass.

THE LAKE'S FAMOUS SCHOOLERS

Schools of bass form between March and October to prey on the shad that roam the surface. Schools of threadfin shad serenely scoot along the surface until busted by the hungry bass. Then, they will reform and continue their migration as though nothing has happened.

The shad are larger here, and much of the schooling activity occurs in relatively deep water in and around massive hydrilla beds. The deep water vegetation serves as the summer holding areas for the lake's larger bass. Feeding activity often draws big fish out from their hiding places for a jealous lunge at whatever they find. An angler catching school bass may come up with the surprise and thrill of his lifetime, thanks to a trophy mixed in with the school. The school-sized bass are real guerrilla fighters; they attack from cover quickly, in small groups and get back down before you can cast to them. Care must be taken to match the bait size and shape to the forage these bass are taking. Lures retrieved quickly through their feeding frenzy will produce a strike, often leading to limit catches. Crankbaits resembling shad will often fool the bass that are temporarily on the surface.

WHERE TO LOOK

Some of the better areas on the north end of Orange Lake include the hydrilla and pads north of 20 Brothers in the River Styx area, the pads around the small islands of vegetation and a slight bottom depression lying off one of the islands. The latter is productive for trollers and jig tossers in the coldest winter and hottest summer months.

The maidencane weedline at Grassy Point holds bass year around, as does a 12-foot deep slot between Cow Hammock and Sampson Point. Trollers of crankbaits, spoonplugs and big shiners often do well along the 10-foot breakline in this depression. Other good areas on the northern half of the lake include a small depression and a large bed of lily pads in 3 to 5 feet of water off Cow Hammock, the isolated brush located approximately midway between Boardman and Samson Point, and the east edge of Samson Point.

There are lots of good places to bass fish in the southwest corner of the lake. The pads and hydrilla off Cow Hammock Point, the lily pads surrounding Redbird Island, the boat channel and a 9 to 10 foot deep depression west of Redbird Island all produce largemouth bass. Also fish the west and north sides of the deep hole off the Heagy-Burry ramp for consistent bass catches. The grass and bonnets around Bird Island and other places near deep water are prime spots to fish in the spring. In fact, fishery biologists have found about 29 pounds of bass per acre of lily pads and about 44 pounds of bass per acre of maidencane in the lake.

The hydrilla point east of Heagy-Burry Park and the northern side of McCormick Island are good producers of bass in the spring. The area east of McCormick Island in Cabbage Cove is productive for fall bass. Isolated pads that lie in slightly deeper water away from the shallow beds hold concentrations of largemouth. Bass also hold on the point northwest of the Gator Hole, the points in P.G. Run, and the Cane Hammock point. When the Cross Creek water is high, the docks can also be productive.

LAKE DETAILS

This Alachua County lake lies about 17 miles southeast of Gainesville. It is connected to Lake Lochloosa via Cross Creek, a canopied, one-mile-long waterway. The area was first made famous in books written by Marjorie Kinnan Rawlings in the 1920s. "The Yearling" and "Cross Creek" were later used as a basis for a movie. Orange Lake is the largest in northeast Florida and encompasses 12,706 acres.

Orange Lake averages about 5 1/2 feet in depth and is approximately 9 miles long by 4 miles wide. Actual acreage and depths depend upon the water table, which fluctuates widely. The lake receives its water from Newnans Lake through River Styx and from Lake Lochloosa through Cross Creek. Drainage is through Orange Creek into the Oklawaha River at Rodman Reservoir.

There are three named islands, McCormick, Redbird and Bird, in the lake. The latter originally developed as a floating island but is now firmly rooted to the bottom. Over the years, Orange Lake has been blessed with the unique phenomenon of such floating islands which typically support abundant stands of vegetation with roots penetrating a dense, peat-like matrix of decaying plant matter.

Throughout history, the spring-fed lakes have had seasonal water problems. A drought in 1977 severely affected the fishery, and in the early 1980s, an influx of hydrilla practically choked the lake. During some years, only airboats and small johnboats were able to navigate the lake. The rampant hydrilla has now been reduced to manageable conditions, creating a "new" fishery. The amount and type of cover today is influenced by aquatic weed control practices, water level fluctuation and time of year. Today, hydrilla occupies about 2,850 acres, sawgrass about 450 acres and water hyacinth just over 100 acres.

There are two public launch areas on the lake. On the northeast end of the Orange Lake off Highway 325 near the Cross Creek inlet is the popular Marjorie Rawlings Park, and on the southwestern shore off Highway 441 at the village of Orange Lake is the Heagy-Burry Park Recreation Area.

19

2

LAKE LOCHLOOSA'S
CANOPY BASS

THE SURFACE EXPLODED beside the hyacinth patch and our boat rocked. I stood and waited for the line to tighten before setting the hook. The bass headed to the deep, only to become entangled in the hyacinth roots dangling around it.

I slowly pulled the bass, along with a small clump of vegetation toward me, while my partner readied the net. The floating plants split as the seven pounder erupted through them. Quick net work by Dan Thurmond saved the bass as the hook popped out of its mouth. We placed the fish in the livewell for photos to be taken later that morning.

I rebaited with an eight-inch long shiner, adjusted the bobber and lobbed the bait to the edge of the vegetation. The native shiner dove quickly under the canopy and tugged the cork back into the darkness. Another bass apparently saw the commotion and quickly grabbed the forage fish. Then he moved slowly away, deeper into the cover.

Few other waters in this country produce as many lunker bass each year!

"Don't let her go too far," my guide friend suggested, as I set back hard on the Series One graphite rod. "There's some thick pad stems under there."

The rod bowed and the hook-up felt solid, but the bass wasn't moving and neither was my reel gaining any line. I put additional pressure on the 40 pound test "mean" green Trilene and the entanglement moved toward me. The line held, as I steadily worked the bass and a couple of pad stems back to the boat. The bass weighed six pounds and the pads about two, it seemed.

21

The prime big bass water on Lake Lochloosa consists of lily pads inundated with floating water hyacinths.

My guide friend and I landed two smaller bass from the hyacinth canopy without even moving the boat. We were thinking about trying another bed of floating cover when another bass of about five pounds struck a lively bait. We stayed another hour and caught three more bass from the very same spot off Lake Lochloosa's south shore. That was one of our many active and fun days on the lake.

Perhaps Thurmond's most interesting catch on the lake was the fish he once caught with the help of an osprey. He watched an osprey coming after one of his cork-positioned shiners and quickly jerked on the rod, trying to make the baitfish dive below the surface and out of the impending 'strike' zone. Dan's attempt failed as the osprey grabbed the shiner and began flying off.

The bird lost its grasp, though, and the struggling shiner fell back into the water. The shiner disappeared and the cork along with him. "Look at that fool," thought Dan to himself. "He's scared to death." He laughed, but stopped when the cork failed to bob back to the surface.

Line peeled from the reel and Dan quickly engaged it and set the hook. The osprey had found Dan his biggest largemouth of that day, a 12 pound, 12 ounce specimen.

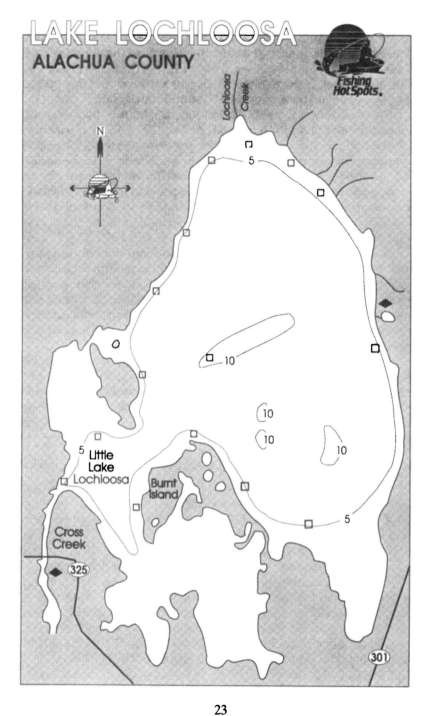

LAKE LOCHLOOSA
ALACHUA COUNTY

Fishing HotSpots.

N

Lochloosa Creek

5

10

10

10

10

5

Little Lake Lochloosa

Burnt Island

Cross Creek

325

5

301

The best time to seek such trophy bass on Lochloosa is from January through June. Statistically, March is the number one month for producing lunker fish, with April ranking second. Thurmond prefers to fish Lochloosa's south end in the spring, moving to the northeast shoreline later on in the fall.

On two different days, Thurmond caught two fish over 12 pounds from the lake. On one day, he had the two giants before 9 a.m. and left before a lot of the fishing crowd arrived. The lake produces lots of huge bass each year, and there is tremendous fishing pressure from anglers. Boat traffic from other types of users is minimal, but the weekend days are particularly crowded. It's not uncommon to find yourself sitting in a spot with over 100 boats fishing nearby. As a result, it is wise to go during the week when the bass are less pressured.

In the spring, Lochloosa is often considered the best big bass lake in Florida. The large amount of hydrilla and other cover has helped the bass population explode. Production over the past few years has increased by 20-fold. Studies by Florida's Game and Fresh Water Fish Commission show that the lake's hydrilla harbors approximately 37 pounds of bass per acre and its lily pad beds about 20 pounds of largemouth per acre.

I have fished the lake often since 1973 and know of no other that produces so many lunker largemouth. Many area guides spend much of their late spring days on the lake, watching lively baits swim back under the green canopies. They have caught several bass up to 15 1/2 pounds by submarining 6 to 10-inch shiners under the floating cover.

TACTICS, LURES & BAIT

Perhaps the most productive technique for giant Lochloosa bass involves a shiner hooked near the anal fin with a 5/0 weedless hook. The bait, trailing a small foam float and 25 to 40-pound test line, is "run" under the floating mats of hyacinths. A float is often used so that the angler can detect a strike easier. It also helps reveal which direction the bass may be going after it strikes.

The prime vegetation is normally found near deep water on the outside edges of lily pads. Flip the shiner to within a foot or so of the flotsam and then urge it to swim back under the canopy. When the baitfish swims far back into the shadows, pay close attention to the line to detect its nervous anxiety and a strike. Eruptions often occur under the canopy as a large bass attacks the shiner.

24

Another very effective tactic to locate fish is to troll shiners over eight feet of water, so that the bass can use the entire water column to feed. In the springtime, you can also wind-drift the baits over deeper water. When the breeze moves the boat too fast to fish effectively, or the boat moves away from the submerged hydrilla beds, it's time to motor back up to the original spot.

During the summer months, trolling crankbaits or in-line spinners along dropoffs or in the deep water slots can be effective. Also tossing injured-minnow plugs in and around the dense cover is productive. Try to fish waters at least four feet deep for larger average weight catch.

When the bass aren't found in the middle of the dense vegetation, concentrate on more open areas. Check out the small islands of heavily matted hydrilla in the early fall. When the sun gets up, bigger largemouth will often move tighter to the small areas of extra-heavy cover. Waters 6 foot deep will hold early spring bass, while summer fish can be found more often in 8 to 9 foot depths.

FOOD FOR THOUGHT

Active bass may be in thinner areas of cover, in open pockets or cuts or in slightly shallow water. When they quit feeding, they will usually move into the thick, vegetated areas. That may be a good time to flip a worm in the dense habitat. Regulars here use dark-colored plastics. During high water, the cut behind the maidencane and pads can be productive for lure tossers.

Abundant crayfish hide under cypress tree roots during daylight hours and explore the bottom after hours. The incredibly poor eyesight of the nocturnal feeder makes it a prime target for the larger predators. Live crayfish and artificials that resemble them are effective bass baits all year long on Lochloosa.

Fish plastic worms slowly in the pad cover for best spring action. Tossing vibrating plugs and spinnerbaits in the summer can be productive on bass holding on the edges of the pads.

Use vibrating lures during mid-day and minnow plugs early and late around isolated patches of hydrilla for maximum action. Troll crankbaits above the weed growth on the bottom or drift plastic worms along the dropoff for additional action.

Fishermen who know the lake's lunkers use 17 to 20 pound test line and sturdy baitcasting reels. Shiner fishermen usually cast 20 to 40 pound test monofilament on these vegetated waters. When a bass is hooked, it usually knows how to use the weeds to its advantage. Be prepared and you'll not be sorry.

Few other waters produce as many giant largemouth per acre each year, but tremendous fishing pressure has taken its toll on the fishery. Most local guides, fish camps and marinas are now encouraging voluntary catch and release to preserve the trophy bass fishing success.

WHERE TO LOOK

There are three important considerations when fishing Lake Lochloosa: the amount and location of hydrilla growth, whether the lake has recently been sprayed for vegetation and the wind strength and direction.

On windy days, explore the upwind edges of hyacinths over seven foot depths. Baitfish are blown out of the near shore pad and hydrilla cover by the weather. After a late spring front, search for the heaviest concentrations of hydrilla with a hyacinth canopy in nine or 10 feet of water and submarine shiners for the best results.

Some of the best areas for year around bass fishing are scattered about the lake. The edges of the northernmost pad field near the small feeder creeks, the hydrilla and mixture of other vegetation off "Old Carraway Landing" near where Lochloosa Creek empties into the lake, the maidencane grassline on the northwestern shoreline, and the edges of vegetation on the northeast shore are all productive bass spots.

A large depression or "slot" in the middle of the lake has a drop of only a couple of feet, but it can hold plenty of trophy-size largemouth during the temperature extremes of summer and winter. Search for the depression with sonar, then troll or spray cast the area for results. The bottom of the slots may have some hydrilla growth which enhances the area's attraction to largemouth.

In the spring and fall, turn to the abundant vegetation along the north shore of Burnt Island. Other great bass areas are along the eastern shoreline and on the southern and southwestern side inside the weedline between the grass and cypress tree perimeter.

The bay off the main lake known as Little Lochloosa is a prime late spring spot for giant largemouth, especially near the holes and pockets in the huge bonnet fields. This spot offers more pads and surface cover than any other. In the pads off the northwest perimeter of Burnt Island are often schooling bass, and in the pads off Allen Point are larger bass. The open water area at the mouth

An eight-inch long shiner is often hooked through the lips and trolled through the submergent vegetation lying just off the floating cover on Lake Lochloosa.

of Cross Creek in 3 to 5 feet of water yields many big bass, as does the hydrilla that lies in front of the lily pads and fish attractor markers.

LAKE DETAILS

Located in Marion County between Highways 301 and 441, Lake Lochloosa is connected to Orange Lake by Cross Creek, a canopied, one-mile-long waterway. The 5,600 acre lake has a maximum depth of 11 feet and an average depth of 7 feet. It stretches about 5 miles north to south and has an average width of 2 1/2 miles.

A large drainage area to the north supplies water into Lochloosa through Lochloosa Creek. Most of the flow leaves the lake through Cross Creek, while some water drains slowly to Orange Creek through Lochloosa Slough in the southeastern corner of the lake.

The lake is home to numerous cypress trees and a variety of aquatic vegetation. Control programs have a major impact on the plant community. Hydrilla became established in Lochloosa in 1974 and at one time covered 65 percent of the lake. Applications of herbicides during the spring is typically done on a series of small plots every other year, and has effectively reduced the plant's growth.

While the amount of aquatic plants varies considerably from year to year, hydrilla remains moderately abundant. The latest figures revealed almost 3,000 acres of hydrilla on the lake. The abundant vegetation harbors grass shrimp and shiners which are great forage. In recent years, the lake has had its share of drought problems. Low waters make access and navigation difficult. The only public launch ramp on the east shore is off highway 301 at SE 162 Avenue in the small community of Lochloosa. During low waters, a 4-wheel drive vehicle may be necessary. In addition to this access, there are a few resort/fish camp landing facilities on Lochloosa and Cross Creek and both public and commercial ramps on sister Lake Orange.

Each of four state fish attractors in Lake Lochloosa covers an area of approximately 100 feet by 100 feet. The locations are generally in open water and are marked by floating buoys painted white, black and orange. Only sunshine bass have been stocked in Lake Lochloosa. Guide service is available through many sources including Dan Thurmond's Guide Service, P.O. Box 313, Orange Springs, FL 32182, phone (904)867-1565.

3

ALACHUA'S MULTI-SPECIES OFFERINGS

ONE OF THE MOST exciting fish in Florida's aquatic environment is a bully! The sunshine bass, or hybrid striped bass, will do things his way or not at all. This "man-made" fish is forceful and explosive, and his popularity on Newnans Lake rivals the largemouth.

Cool weather is the time to catch the sunshine on Newnans. Many anglers are, however, just beginning to discover the thrill of catching these battlers. Fortunately, this lake is one of the best bets for catching several sunshine bass.

There are actually two types of hybrid bass. The parents of both types are the fresh water white bass and their originally saltwater kin, the striped bass. Stripers have been acclimating themselves to freshwater for many years and originally were land-locked in South Carolina's Santee Cooper reservoir, where they became well established.

Both sunshine bass and largemouth offer great cool weather action in Gainesville area waters!

A successful stocking program of that species was conducted by several of the southern states' fish and game departments, including Florida's Game and Fresh Water Fish Commission. Results of those stocking efforts in the St. Johns, Apalachicola and St. Mary's Rivers were quite encouraging, and survival of the fingerlings was reasonably good. The striper is, however, somewhat temperamental in its feeding habits.

The striper's growth has been satisfactory mainly in the larger, deeper bodies of water, but few Florida anglers appeared inter-

29

ested or capable of catching the fish. Thus, a need still existed for a popular, fast-growing and easy-to-catch species that could aid in shad predation.

South Carolina successfully developed the hybrid striper, a cross between a male white bass and a female striped bass, in 1965. The breed was easier to catch than the striper and grew rapidly. Florida soon began experimenting with the hybrid and began stocking the fish in 1972.

Results of the experiment were successful, and today several of those hybrids still roam Florida waters. That fish, however, is not to be confused with the sunshine bass which was experimentally developed in 1973. The sunshine bass is a cross between a striper male and a white bass female, and Florida was the only state to successfully introduce that cross breed into fresh waters.

On Newnans and other waters in the state, the sunshine bass roams a different area than the largemouth and generally does not compete with them for forage. They travel in schools and are extremely aggressive. Their growth rate has been fantastic in some waters and the state record now stands at 15 pounds, 10 ounces.

The hybrids are very tough from a fish culture point of view; they are easy to produce and handle, and their survival is excellent. Over two million sunshines are stocked annually in 174,000 acres of lakes and 430 miles of rivers throughout Florida. The sterile hybrid is a put and take fishery in Newnans and other waters, but the future is definitely bright for the fish.

IDENTIFICATION AND FORAGE

Newnans Lake does not have stripers or white bass, so identification is relatively simple. The hybrid possesses certain physical characteristics of each of its parents, but probably resembles the striped bass more than the white bass. Lateral stripes on the hybrid are prominent (similar to the striped bass) but they are broken. The hybrid is a deeper-bodied fish than the striper. It is silvery in coloration with a bluish hue along his back and black lateral side stripes.

The fish has a definite food preference and tops on the list is shad. He usually prefers the bite-size threadfin shad that frequent Newnans' open water areas. The larger sunshine bass do eat shad that may outgrow crappie and other smaller species which also inhabit open water areas.

Although Newnans' sunshines are open water fish, they are very structure-oriented. They move to their primary food source,

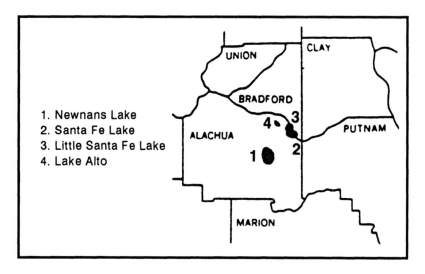

1. Newnans Lake
2. Santa Fe Lake
3. Little Santa Fe Lake
4. Lake Alto

the shad, along deep water paths. They will feed on the shad at any depth, and schools of the hybrids will chase their forage right to the surface.

The hapless shad have little defense against their aggressive predators. The raging hybrids will maim and kill multitudes of shad daily and will constantly 'pig-out' on the morsels. Once stuffed, the sunshines will descend to bottom structure to rest, digest and await another shad school.

A hybrid's plump belly has little effect on its fighting ability, however, and it can move like a freight train. A hefty hybrid will give an angler the fight of his life, guaranteed. As with many of their salt water relatives, they are faster, stronger and have more stamina than many of the fresh water game fish.

TACTICS, LURES & BAITS

Structure fishing patterns can be established and either casting or trolling techniques can be productive most times of the year. When Newnans' sunshine bass are schooling and popping the shad at the top, then surface tactics can be used to advantage.

The fish have a definite lure preference for white, silver or gold colored baits. For casting, threadfin shad-resembling plugs and bucktail or maribou jigs are hard to beat. White or yellow grubs are deadly, as are the heavy slab spoons and tail spinner baits. Trolling favorites such as Hellbenders and Bombers are the usual fare, and a fast troll has proved productive. Lightweight spoons and spinners, as well as topwater plugs, can be productive in a thrashing school of surface feeders.

Any lure that resembles a shad and approximates the size of forage that the hybrids are feeding on has potential. Summer angling on Newnans Lake finds jigs and tail spinners to be preferred by successful anglers. The hybrids are usually found in open water around changes (even minimal) in depth. Worked near the bottom, 1/2-ounce jigs and slab spoons can take a quick limit. Slabs weighing up to one ounce and painted white can be effective when jigged over productive structures found on the chart recorder. These heavy baits can be yo-yoed over dropoffs and points.

Hybrid schools may move to the surface chasing shad in the summer, and an angler can have a ball tossing topwater plugs, such as one of the thin minnow lures, into the activity. Sunshine bass are light-sensitive and generally move shallower on cloudy days to feed. Bright sun rays which penetrate the tannic-stained water will usually drive the fish down. Early morning, late evening, windy and rainy days can all be highly productive, as the larger hybrids can be located nearer the surface.

A dynamic lure duo which is successful on hybrids consists of a large, deep-diving crankbait and a small white jig attached about two feet behind the lure. The treble hook on the tail of the plug can be removed for ease of handling since the trailer will account for most of the action. A slower troll with this rig is preferred by the hybrid experts.

A final productive method to fool some of Newnans' sunshine bass is by drifting minnows or other forage fish over humps or bottom irregularities. Even live shiners will produce well when dropped into deep holes, and shad have produced some real whoppers.

Newnans is a eutrophic lake with highly enriched waters and a thriving population of the cross breeds. A good chart recorder or sonar unit, a handful of deep diving plugs, and an extra large net are all that are required for this game fish. Bass anglers have a dual opportunity on this lake: largemouth in and around the cover and sunshine bass in open water.

NEWNANS FOR BASS

Newnans Lake is a 7,427-acre lake of tannic-stained water just east of Gainesville. It is about 3 1/2 miles long and two miles wide. The lake is ringed by cypress trees draped in Spanish moss, and

Newnans Lake is a very productive bass spot during the winter months.

many grow 25 yards or so from land into the lake's shallows. Vegetation in the form of hydrilla and aquatic grass surrounds the knees of the bass-holding trees in the late summer. The shallows taper off slowly toward the depths which reach to 10 or 12 feet in most areas. Some gradual dropoffs "plummet" to 15 feet in places, and some plug trollers catch some big bass in the hotter months, but the majority of largemouth are taken in shallower water.

Some minor humps exist in the depths, and these hold bass in the winter and summer months. Points of vegetation off Palm and

Kennedy Points and the near-shore cover at the mouths of Gum Root and Hatchet Creek yield spring largemouth. While some lunkers up to 14 pounds have been taken, the largest I've seen taken here was a respectable 10-pound, 8-ounce specimen. It was pulled from the western shoreline during the coldest of winter days.

The flooded cypress trees yield plenty of bass, particularly if the wind is blowing into them. Baitfish seem to be pushed into those windward shallows, and the bass are quick to feed on the offering. Lily pad beds on the lake's perimeter also hold bass in cooler times and seasons. Check them out in the mornings and evenings during the hottest months, the early afternoon in the winter and any time the rest of the year.

SANTA FE CHALLENGE

This 4,721-acre Santa Fe Lake near the town of Waldo is often overlooked by serious bass anglers; it shouldn't be. The lake with heavily developed shoreline offers excellent largemouth fishing at times, and yields some trophy specimens ever year. Part of a three-lake chain, the waters are easy to fish and they offer year around action. The 540-acre Lake Alto (also spelled "Altho" on some sources), and the 1,135-acre Little Santa Fe Lake are connected by short canals to the bigger lake, and they also produce good bass fishing.

The waters here are usually clear, and the depths offer submerged vegetation. The shoreline cover is in the form of maidencane and cypress trees, and for those stealthy anglers, that's where the early action may take place. Springtime fishing with live shiners or giant worms are effective means to catch a monster largemouth. You might not break the lake's 16-pound record, but you could get close.

Sandbars and humps lie 200 yards off the perimeter shoreline of the big lake, and that is where wise bassmen will concentrate their efforts in the summer and winter. The water depth is between 7 and 14 feet deep in many of these areas. Troll the live bait along the drops or drag a Texas- or Carolina-rigged worm over the sandy bottom. A deep-running crankbait can be productive early in the morning nearer the grassy perimeter at times. Also concentrate on brush piles when you can find them for mid-day action.

Fishing the docks and piers around the lake, particularly at night, can be productive. Many have lights on them which attract

Numerous 10 and 11 pound bass come from Alachua County's picturesque waters.

bugs and small forage fish. Bassing the cooler hours after dark should prove successful on this lake. Buzz-baits, topwater plugs and plastic worms are a summer selection that will prove effective. In the fall, look for some schooling bass action, and toss them Rat-L-Traps or tail-spinner lures.

A good ramp lies on Santa Fe Lake off highway 26, about two miles west of Melrose. Access to Little Santa Fe Lake is on the east side of highway 21B. Both can accommodate regular 2-wheel drive cars when the water level is normal.

4

ST. JOHNS MONSTER BASS

SHORT-STOPPING your plastic worms is their trick. Crabs seem to love the imitation wigglers. Yes, fishing this section of the river is interesting. Sure, it's productive, providing some of the state's best largemouth and striped bass fishing. But dealing with the saltwater influence makes this fishing different. Tides that leave shallow canals almost dry and marine species with teeth are what you may come across in the waters between Jacksonville and Palatka.

I was fishing Doctors Lake just off the mighty St. Johns, where the bass were thick in the piers between the lake and main river channel. I lost several good fish on the barnacle-clad pilings, but the lesson taught me to use heavy line and tackle. The fish had not wrapped the line around the dock posts but the line had severed by touching the pilings. The day did prove a worthwhile

Crabs, shrimp, barnacles and fish with teeth are on the docket ... for the big river's largemouth action!

venture, however, as my two companions and myself caught and released over 45 pounds of largemouth from pilings and docks. Two of our catch would have weighed almost 8 pounds each.

Bass in the watershed's piers and docks are usually found shallower than you would normally expect them to be in most lakes. Food, cover and protection are what bass demand, and the St. Johns River docks and piers provide it. In fact, I have so much confidence in this type of structure that my first target on waters along the St. Johns is any pier, dock or pilings that project above the surface.

Fish houses on the ends of wooded piers provide good bass action on Doctors Lake, south of Orange Park. The challenge is to determine a largemouth bite from that of a crab.

Bass love to hang out around wood structure. The pilings in Doctors Lake and those along the St. Johns on either side have produced some monster bass. Bulkheads and docks throughout the entire river hold largemouth year around, providing excellent cover, forage and protection. Crayfish frequent the rotting wood posts and feed on microscopic organisms found beneath piers. Shade is abundant in these areas, and the water temperature can be slightly cooler and richer in oxygen.

TACTICS & LURES

Piers and pilings along the river system come in all shapes, sizes, lengths and conditions. Many near Jacksonville even have small cabins on the end several hundred feet from shore. Many are partially dilapidated, while others have brand new unweathered pilings and cross members.

The best pier under which to locate river bass will depend on several things, but the most important criteria is how close it is to deep water. Remember, deep water is relative to the type of water you're fishing. It could be six feet on Doctors Lake and 18 feet along an outer bend of Black Creek. If it doesn't have this requirement, then your chances of finding bass under that dock are minimized.

38

The piers on which small houses are built, between Green Cove Springs and Mandarin on the St. Johns, provide excellent bass fishing. The wider piers which cast a wider shadow are prime territories all along the watershed. A long, skinny pier in shallow water is often a waste of time. Usually, the deeper water and more protection a pier offers the bass, the better the fishing opportunity will be. The density and size of the support posts beneath the pier is always an important consideration. The more dense (number of posts, cross-members near the water, etc.) the more productive a pier can be. The larger in diameter that these posts are, the better they usually prove to be also.

Another consideration in determining which dock to fish in this section of the St. Johns is the algae and barnacle growth on the supports. The more the better your chances are of finding a bass home. Pilings and piers can hold summer bass for a couple of hours or forever, depending on the availability of food and deep water.

When it's hot, largemouth bass activity will be under the deeper docks and around deeper vegetated areas. Higher pH levels in shallow waters cause an adjustment to slightly deeper waters, as well as to more shaded waters and to those in current. Fish submerged trees lying on the bottom of deep outer bends in the tributaries or the St. Johns. Check out the bars, points and dropoffs found by sonar with a deep-running crankbait or bottom-bumping plastic bait, like a Carolina-rigged worm. During the hottest months, the Berkley Power Worm fished beside pilings and docks and in submerged brush is probably the most productive lure for monster-size river largemouth.

Other productive lures on the river are white and gray-hued crankbaits and vibrating plugs. Selection of such should depend on the current and depth. When the river area is deep or contains a fast current, you may have to get your lure down to work the productive area nearest the runoff. Many anglers toss the deep running billed baits. If the river current is not extremely fast, there is time to work the lures deeper in search of the larger bass.

BRACKISH WATER BAIT

The St. Johns brackish water offers a productive technique not common in inland lakes nearby. During summer shrimp spawning runs, juvenile shrimp migrate from the sea into the river, and the largemouth go on a three or four week feeding binge. The shrimp run usually starts in June and lasts through the summer.

Boat docks, piers, and bridges are the favorite hotspots. The boat is generally positioned up-current from a pier or dock and the shrimp is drifted into and under the structure. A bobber aids in controlling the presentation. Many of the bassmen in the area use cane poles equipped with 15-feet of 30-pound test monofilament in order to haul out lunker bass from the barnacle-covered terrain. A small treble hook, a couple of split shot, and a frisky saltwater shrimp complete the rig.

The shrimp are hooked through the head below the horn for best results, and fished about a foot off the bottom. Flipping the morsel under a dock or pier is easy with the long pole and the leverage and heavy line come in handy while extracting heavyweight largemouth from the structure. Fishing shrimp for largemouth bass is probably the easiest method to use in the summer months, and the most productive!

SUMMER SCHOOL BASS

Some summer bass move into the depths and then surface to explode on a school of threadfin shad. The baitfish activity is normally peaking in August, with the greatest occurrence of algae blooms taking place. Largemouth schoolers are aware of this and certainly take advantage of the situation. Often, the St. Johns bass schools will stuff themselves on shad in open water and then move into the man-made timber to relax.

Schooling bass can be found around the deeper channels where tributaries enter or leave the river, where the St. Johns enters or leaves a lake or slough, and, sometimes, at wide spots in the river during the late summer and fall. The bass are most likely to be breaking water just before afternoon thunderstorms. Many St. Johns bass chasers head to the mouths of tributaries where the water clarity may be different from the river.

A productive way to fish the deeper schools is to stay downstream in the larger water and cast up into the smaller tributary. The banks should be worked carefully, casting parallel to them and varying the depth of the retrieve. Cast the center of the tributary's mouth thoroughly with deep running lures for top action.

Selection of a schooler lure is important. While these fish may work into such a frenzy that they'll hit about anything, more often the best strings of St. Johns schoolers will be taken on baits resembling shad, on shiners and on other soft-rayed forage.

Especially productive are white and gray-hued lures and popular Color C-Lector schemes, depending on localized conditions. The river school bass normally chase small shad, so smaller lures are more effective.

Lure selection should depend on the current and depth. When the river area is deep or contains a fast current, you may have to get your lure down to work the productive area nearest the runoff. Many prefer vibrating lures, and Bill Lewis' Rat-L-Trap and Storm's Texas Shad are good choices. If the river current is not extremely fast there is time to work the lures deeper in search of the larger bass. A diver such as Norman's Deep Little "N" may be the ticket.

GIANT BASS OPPORTUNITIES

The St. Johns River produces a lot of giant largemouth bass, but one taken in April a few years ago by Jacksonville angler, Buddy Wright, is the biggest ever from these waters. In fact, the largemouth, weighing 18 pounds, 13 ounces, is probably the Sunshine State's biggest bass captured in the past 30 years, and the third largest ever caught in Florida.

Wright was tossing a Norman Weed Walker II and retrieving the topwater spoon over eel grass beds in three feet of water near Green Cove Springs. The largemouth struck the frog-colored bait right at the boat and peeled off several feet of Wright's 14 pound test line. The fish soon became buried in the dense vegetation, but careful handling by the 41-year old angler worked her free. At boat-side, Wright first grabbed the giant by the tail and then the lip to swing her aboard.

The late afternoon catch measured 29 1/2 inches in length and 26 1/2 inches in girth. Wright, a confirmed lunker hunter with panhandle bass of 13 and 15 pounds to his credit, had only fished this area of the river once before. He was using spinning tackle and fishing from a johnboat with 4 hp outboard.

Wright chose the unique paddle-wheel spoon "because of its ability to move over and through the grass and because it's a good big bass bait." On his first cast that evening, he caught a five pounder. On the fifth, he put the record monster in the boat and headed for the scales at a local grocery store.

With oceanic tides reaching upstream nearly 100 miles and numerous salt springs discharging into the river, the St. Johns supports a diverse fishery of both freshwater and marine species.

Buddy Wright of Jacksonville, caught this 18-pound 13-ounce largemouth from the St. Johns River near Green Cove Springs in 1989. It is Florida's biggest bass in modern times.

The southernmost indigenous population of striped bass in the world resides in the St. Johns River right next to some giant largemouth. This area contains numerous ten-pound largemouth bass, and many stripers exceeding that weight.

Supplemental striped bass stocking began in 1970 and hybrid striped bass have been stocked since 1981. Few stripers exceed 25 pounds in this section of the St. Johns due to their shorter growing season and increased physical stress resulting from elevated water temperatures. In fact, without cool water refuges and the present stocking rates employed, a severe reduction in their lifespan and total population in this section of the St. Johns would be inevitable.

Striper hot spots in this section of the river during the summer include the deep waters of Black Creek. Late winter and spring concentrations of stripers occur at the railroad bridge in Jacksonville and at the Interstate 295 bridge (Buckman Bridge) just south of the city. Other prime striper locations on the river include the pilings of all major bridges, feeder-creek mouths and the deep river channels between lakes. Rat-L Traps, in-line spinners, shad-resembling crankbaits, live shiners and 1/2 to 1 ounce white or yellow jigs are best bets to fool a striped bass.

WHERE TO LOOK FOR BASS

From Palatka northward, the St. Johns River is more like a lake, often widening to a couple of miles. The waters are tidal influenced from here to the mouth and the current can be strong or even reversed, depending on the lunar phase, winds and tides. Some places in the river will produce largemouth bass on an incoming tide, while others will yield best on an outgoing tide. The tide controls the forage; when it is going out, it pulls the bait out of the grassbeds, out of the creeks and sloughs, and when running in, it pushes the forage up into those areas.

A "dead" tide will usually kill the bass activity. The key when this happens is to keep moving until you find some moving water. With a river in some places four miles wide, that may take some doing. Fishing the tides, particularly in the winter, is vital to catching bass in this section of the St. Johns. Find the current and deep water in the tributaries and fish the steepest banks and sharpest dropoffs. Creeks, canals, and sloughs along the St. Johns in this area produce well, particularly during moderate weather. Grass beds and manmade wood are attractions to largemouth here too.

Low water levels concentrate bass and other game fish in the deeper river sections. Fortunately, submerged vegetation, like eelgrass, is not normally affected by water level changes. Huge expanses of eelgrass flats are where the bass often forage. When you can find such cover, that is where to fish. During the spring, most bass will be holding close to the sand-bottom eelgrass beds where spawning takes place. After the spawn, the bass will drop back to structure in deeper water.

Between Black Creek and the Atlantic Ocean are numerous largemouth areas that produce almost year around. The brackish waters in the heart of Jacksonville, like most heavily tidal-influenced waters, are often overlooked by the bass fishing fraternity. The Arlington River, Pottsburg Creek, and others around the mouth of the St. Johns are some of my old, "secret" bass waters. Barnacles and largemouth do mix, and quite nicely.

The upper section of the Ortega River deepens and provides bass a sanctuary from heat, cold and saltwater intrusion. The mussel beds often found off Christopher Point, the weed bed drop on the south side of the Beauclerc Bluff point, the grassy Ragged Point, and the old pilings along the mouth of Julington Creek and canals off of it are all productive spots. Hibernia Point, the sharp dropoff at the marker just off New Switzerland Point, and the mouth of Black Creek are additional spots in the northern part of the river.

Doctors Lake offers great spring and fall bass fishing. The weed edges, dock supports and bridge pilings at the mouth of the lake concentrate largemouth and saltwater redfish (sometimes called red bass). Both sides of Geiger Point, the dropoff at Peoria Point, and one of my favorite spots, Swimming Pen Creek, all offer good largemouth fishing.

Further south on the St. Johns, the eel grass of Magnolia Point, the docks and old submerged pilings off Green Cove Springs, and the grass patches from Kendall Creek north to Orange Grove Branch are top areas to check out for largemouth. The dropoffs found off Smith Point, in Florence Cove and in Palmo Cove, are productive most of the year. Pacetti Point pilings and grass patches are a long-time favorite of area bass chasers. The shallow grass patches in Puerto Rico Cove and Colee Cove are both good bass spots.

Other good largemouth waters north of Palatka can be found at Clark Creek, Willis Point, Racy Point and Tocoi Point. Tocoi Creek, Cedar Creek, and Deep Creek all yield largemouth bass on high, outgoing tides. Federal Point, Masons Creek, Rice Creek and the canals in the area are good springtime bass locations.

The boat docks just north of the Palatka city bridge often yield bass in the fall and winter.

RIVER & LAKE DETAILS

This section of the St. Johns lies in northeast Florida, between the towns of Jacksonville and Palatka and is bordered by Highway 17. The river flows north and dumps an estimated 4 billion gallons of freshwater annually into the Atlantic Ocean. It is the largest river in Florida whose drainage lies entirely within the state. This

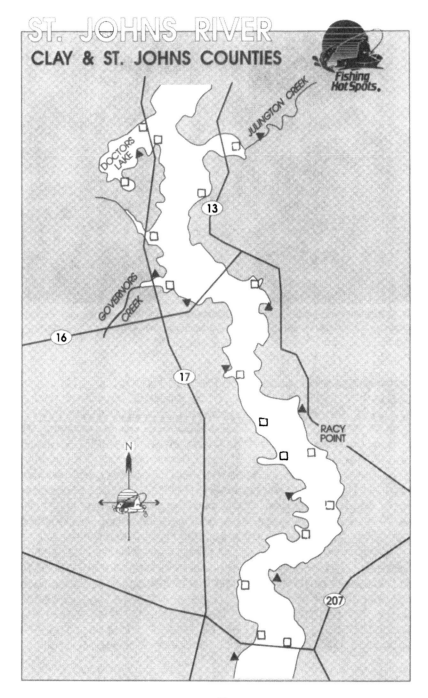

The docks and pilings along the river usually are among the most productive bass structures. Fish them when the waters are warm and when the sun is out for best results.

section of the river encompasses the 3,400-acre Doctors Lake with average depths of about 13 feet. The river itself is slightly estuarine, with sandy shorelines bordering a wide, lagoon-like shallow basin. It has a maximum depth of about 40 feet but averages around 18.

The northward-flowing St. Johns River originates in south central Florida and is typically dark tannic stained; Rice Creek, Trout Creek and Black Creek are tributaries discharging into this section of the river. Julington and Durbin Creeks are among other small tributaries in this area. Hydrilla, eelgrass and southern naiad are submerged vegetation, and water hyacinth, spatterdock and yellow pond lily all can be seen emerging from the surface.

Launch ramps along this section of the river are numerous. Lakeshore Drive is a double-lane concrete ramp on the south side of Doctors Lake off Highway 220; Hood Landing Boat Ramp is on the east side of the river off Highway 13 on Julington Creek. Ramps are also on Governor's Greek on the west side of the river north of Green Cove Springs on Highway 17 and on the west side of the river at Green Cove Springs near the Highway 16 bridge.

On the east side of the river off Highway 13 just south of Six Mile Creek is the Palmo Cove Boat Ramp, and on the west side of the river south of Green Cove Springs is the remote Williams Park Ramp off Highway 209. The launching of large boats at the latter would be difficult. On the east side of the river south of Tocoi off Highway 13 is the Riverdale Park boat ramp. On the west side of the river off Highway 209 and Cedar Creek Road is the Palmetto Bluff Boat Ramp. Another ramp lies on the east side of the river off Highway 207A and East River Road.

Guides on this section of the river include: Terry LaCoss, Amelia Angler, Amelia Island, FL, or phone (904) 261-2870; Bob Stonewater's Trophy Bass Guide Service, 179 Glenwood Rd., DeLand, FL 32720 or phone (904) 736-7120; and Peter Thliveros, North Florida Bass Guides, 1306 S. Edgewood Ave., Jacksonville, FL 32205 or phone (904) 772-7927.

5

LAKE TALQUIN'S RESTORED FISHERY

MY BRIEF CHECKOUT trip after the last drawdown resulted in three bass in the three-pound range. They all came from a short stretch of still-exposed shoreline on the north shore near the dam. The fish were fat and healthy, a typical result of restored habitat and fishery. The brush and newly planted vegetation in Lake Talquin provided great summer fishing that day. In fact, after the past two drawdowns, the bass have gone crazy.

The timbered areas can be spotted emerging from the water's surface or, if they are totally submerged, with the aid of a good map and a good depth finder. These now productive waters have vast areas of submerged timber, although many anglers may not realize it. When water levels increase, evidence of wood may not even pierce the surface, but the wise angler will hunt for it.

New bottom, new vegetation and a booming new fishery have revitalized the Talquin experience!

Lake Talquin is one of the most productive largemouth bass and striped bass lakes in the state, thanks to drawdowns, rehabitation, striper stocking and special fishery management regulations. According to the Florida Game and Fresh Water Fish Commission, the lake is the top winter largemouth bass area in Florida. The area produces almost twice the state's average number of bass caught per hour, making it one of the most popular freshwater fishing areas in Northwest Florida. It is also one of the most beautiful.

Since the impoundment was not cleared prior to flooding, dense cover in the form of submerged hardwood trees, fallen logs, pads and other vegetation are abundant. The flooded timber and submerged stump flats, though, can be a boater's nightmare, so it is advisable to cruise slowly out of the channels and watch the depth finder closely. Because of the recent draining and reflooding of the lake, logs may be partially dried out and partially submerged. It normally takes several months after a drawdown and refill for some of the timber to get waterlogged enough to sink to the bottom.

The dam was utilized for hydroelectric power production until 1970 when title to the dam, reservoir and a portion of the surrounding lands was conveyed to the State of Florida. In 1970, the Department of Natural Resources assumed responsibility for operation and maintenance of the dam and facilities. At that time, the reservoir was designed primarily as a public recreation area. That changed in 1982.

"Florida Power donated the reservoir to the city of Tallahassee," explained a Commission biologist. "There was a stipulation that the lake would be used expressly for recreational activities. Other uses subsequently allowed could not interfere with recreation."

"Thus, Talquin is one of the few lakes in the state that we can draw down without a lot of involved red tape," he continued. "The flexibility we have with this impoundment encouraged us, and from our experimentation also with size restrictions in 1986, we learned a lot."

Those initial harvest regulations required the immediate live release of all largemouth between 11 and 14 inches. Creel surveys conducted during the remainder of that study indicated anglers released slightly over 50% of all bass caught, with the majority within the slot limit. The slot limit restriction lasted through June 1989. Today, a minimum length limit restriction of 14 inches is imposed on Lake Talquin bass.

TACTICS, LURES & BAIT

In the winter, fish the dropoffs and channels. A depth finder is very valuable to locate the best structure and position the boat properly. Anchor in water 6 to 10 feet deep and cast Texas- or Carolina-rigged plastic worms, tail spinner lures or jigs into waters 20 to 30 feet deep. Work them from deep to shallow. Deep diving crankbaits can be trolled to locate action, if you don't mind the occasional hang-up.

During warm spells, fish deep stump flats in 8 to 15 foot depths with vibrating plugs or lipped divers. Largemouth often are

Lake Talquin was drawn down 30 feet and the bottom was allowed to dry. This has brought excellent fishing to the reservoir.

attracted to crankbaits that bump the numerous cover found on Talquin. It is particularly effective when the bass are holding tight to cover. Most of the bass are taken from structures between six and 14 feet deep on the impoundment.

Big bass are occasionally caught and winter months are usually the best to pursue a trophy. The reputed lake record of 16 3/4 pounds was taken in 1970 when the lake had the best habitat of its history. Many largemouth between 10 and 14 pounds were caught then as a result of the 1959 dam restoration drawdown. Today's lunker hunter won't find the catching as easy, but there are still several bass caught each year that weigh between six and 11 pounds.

In the spring, fish the grass flats in 4 to 7 feet of water. Search for areas off the river and creek channels that may provide spawning grounds. Pre spawners will be in the deeper waters at the edge of the flats. Minnow plugs and crankbaits, as well as worms, are effective at the junctions of tributaries. Topwater lures produce in late spring when fished in the shallows near cover. Live shiners are also a good trophy bass producer in the spring.

From April through June, bass jam into the feeder creeks, the back ends of coves and the bays, especially those with lily pads.

Spinnerbaits and buzz baits are effective on the bonnet-loving bass. Weedless spoons with rind trailers are also effective.

The summertime heat offers excellent night fishing along the shoreline and vegetation on the flats. Topwater plugs and weightless worms are productive then. During the day, bass are on deeper structures, in creek and river channel banks and in the limited dense vegetation in shallower waters. Plastic worms, crankbaits and jigging spoons are effective.

Fall patterns often center around the schooling action and migration to deeper waters from the shallows via creek and river channels. Look for the concentrations around the tributary mouths, but these schooling patterns may change from one day to the next. Schoolers are attracted to shad-resembling vibrating baits and shallow-running crankbaits. Usually, the schoolers will feed on shad in the mouth of one creek for 3 or 4 days and then follow the bait to another area. Anglers cashing in on the action have to follow as well.

In the late fall, the schoolers move to the lower end of the lake and tend to hold over deeper water. As the waters cool, structure-oriented largemouth are often caught on minnow lures, vibrating plugs and plastic worms fished in 8 to 12 foot of water in the early fall. Bigger bass are normally caught off ledges along the deep channels. Jigs, spoons and heavy worm rigs are productive.

OCHLOCKONEE RIVER

Suwannee bass can occasionally be taken from Talquin's headwaters, the upper Ochlockonee River. The rare species is a strong fighter and a thrill to catch. They'll hit most anything that resembles a crayfish, which comprises about 90 percent of their diet. Crankbaits, dark jigs with plastic crayfish trailer and other lures whose action and coloration is close to a live crustacean will fool the Suwannee bass. Cast such fare around any limestone outcropping and be ready for a jolt.

The Ochlockonee River originates in south Georgia, meandering southward about 75 miles through the Apalachicola National Forest before ending at Ochlockonee Bay on the Gulf of Mexico near Panacea. Ochlockonee means "yellow river", a Seminole Indian name derived probably from the river's clay-stained color during heavy rains. It provides a 67 mile canoe trail from Highway 20 bridge below the Talquin dam to U.S. 319, near Sopchoppy.

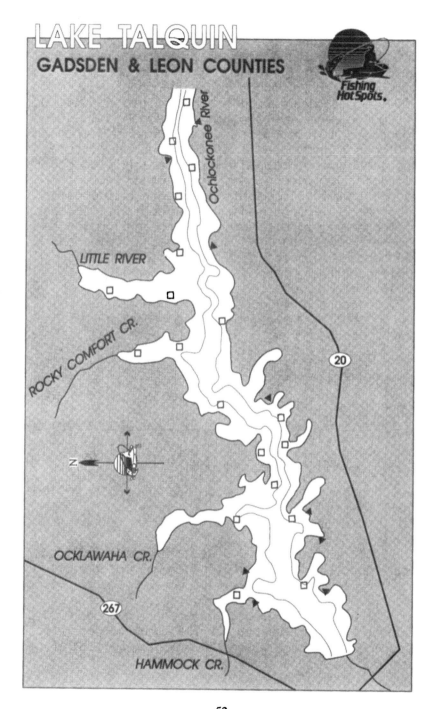

LAKE TALQUIN
GADSDEN & LEON COUNTIES

Fishing Hot Spots.

Ochlockonee River

LITTLE RIVER

ROCKY COMFORT CR.

N

OCKLAWAHA CR.

HAMMOCK CR.

20

267

53

The Ochlockonee has few spring sources. It is composed almost entirely of runoff surface water. In the springtime, flood waters turn this river into a fast flowing waterway, and the fish spread out, making them difficult to locate.

Most of the bass are in or just off the moving water found in the outside river bends, where the water is deeper. The wide, straight stretches of the river are usually not as productive. The best strategy for fishing the river is to fish with the current. That can be done by motoring up from the boat ramp and drifting back down.

The best fishing is found when the river water level has lowered and stabilized, with water still draining from the overflow swamps. This is usually during April, May and June, especially if there have been extended dry periods. The Ochlockonee produces impressive largemouth bass, with 10-pounders quite common at certain times of the year. Big lipped crankbaits are very productive around the numerous fallen logs and sunken tree branches. Plastic worms in black and grape colors, and crayfish imitations are also productive.

There are paved launch sites on both shores of the river, the best are maintained by the U.S. Forest Service at Pine Creek Landing on the upper eastern shore and downriver at Mack Lake and Wood Lake. Ramps located at the end of remote forest roads are at Whitehead Lake, Lower Langston and Hitchcock, but they are undependable during low water. A good map of the river can be obtained from the U.S. Forest Service, P.O. Box 1050, Tallahassee, FL 32302.

STRIPED BASS OPTION

Lake Talquin contains a relatively small, fast growing, but short-lived, population of striped bass which is maintained by annual stockings of fingerlings. The Game and Fresh Water Fish Commission initiated stocking of fingerlings into the lake in 1968 and has continued it annually over the years. Numbers of fish stocked is usually around 200,000.

The lake and the Ochlockonee River tailrace offer good winter/spring striper fishing. On the reservoir, some stripers are taken from Oklawaha Creek during the summer and others from open water in late October and November. Talquin stripers rarely exceed 20 pounds due to the limited thermal refuge (cooler spring water) in the system. Only a couple of 25 pounders have ever been taken, but fish in the 10 to 15 pound class are caught consistently through the fall and winter months.

In the fall, keep a vigilant eye on the surface to detect schooling fish or birds feeding on small baitfish. Both largemouth and striped bass may be feeding on the threadfin shad. Stripers are taken year-round, but they prefer to school and feed vigorously during the cooler months of the year. They will take live bait, such as shad or shiner minnows, quite readily, as well as strike small spinners, shad-resembling plugs and jigs. Since stripers travel in schools and spend much of their time in open water, trolling is also an effective way to locate these schools.

In the winter and early spring, large bass and stripers move up from very deep water in the river channel into the creek fingers on Talquin. Deep-running crankbaits and live shiners are very effective on trophy-size fish then. Striper anglers normally employ heavy bait casting or spinning tackle with lines testing 20 to 30 pounds. The most popular artificial for striped bass is the 1/2 to 1 ounce white or yellow bucktail jig. Size selection on lake waters should be based on the size of the forage the stripers are feeding on and on the depth being fished.

For jump fishing the schools that are feeding on shad, minnow plugs and chugger topwater lures are tops. Either one of the twosome with a small white jig rigged as a trailer one foot behind the plug can be especially effective. Once they sound in the depths, jigging spoons are a good choice. Fishing live bait is a productive method during the hotter months. Fishing with bait minnows at night with a bright light as a fish attractor is also effective, since the fish may be more active then.

Flowing waters attract stripers, and fishing such areas frequently results in fine catches. Many Talquin stripers are caught below the dam in the tailrace using jigs or small shad. The shad can be fished live or dead and are cast and rolled along the bottom to attract both stripers and hybrids. In the tailrace below the Talquin dam, fishermen also adapt to swift current conditions by tossing jigs weighing 3/4 to 1 1/2 ounces that will sink into 15 feet depths quickly.

WHERE TO LOOK

Some of the better areas on the lake are near its headwaters. The Smokehouse area off the mouth of Hunter Creek is a flat about 4 feet deep which offers excellent spring bass fishing. Stumps and other vegetation along the channel offers great cover for forage and bass. Picnic Point is a sand bar in one of the widest sections of the Ochlockonee River before it enters the lake. The bar drops from heavy cover in 5 feet on the rim down to about 22 feet in mid-channel.

In the river headwaters area, the Iron Post area between the mouth of the Ochlockonee and Coe's Landing offers a deep hole at the bend of an old submerged channel. Most submerged river channel bends in the Coe's Landing area are prime largemouth spots. Another great spot is a small creek channel beside Coe's Landing at the southern tip of the Iron Curtain. A lot of bass hold on the excellent dropoff from the tiny creek's sandbars.

The deep channel upstream from High Bluff Landing provides excellent winter angling, as does the creek channel that runs from Double Creek to an old wooden pile-supported pier. Old docks between Coe's and Williams Landings provide excellent bass fishing, and so does the far western side of the mouth of the Little River near where the channel passes. Schooling bass work through the flats adjacent to the channel during the summer. This is also one of the most consistent striped bass schooling areas on Talquin. A good year around schooling largemouth bass area is where Hewes Creek and the Ochlockonee River channel merges.

In the mid-lake area, The mouth of Harvey Creek offers striped bass and white bass in the fall. Waters 5 to 7 feet deep toward the back of Rocky Comfort Creek and those in the back of the Little River arm of the lake provide excellent bass fishing in the spring. The area from Judge's Point off Rocky Comfort Creek west to Gainey's Talquin Lodge offers good year around bass action.

The area southwest of Goat Island is a productive largemouth spot in the early spring. Spawning bass will move into the shallow flats behind the island and on the point opposite the island. You can find the same in the back of the clear Oklawaha Creek where waters drop to 10 feet at the back of the cove near the old mill dam. The waters of the Oklawaha Creek are clearer and cooler than others around the lake. As a result, big striped bass are often caught from the mouth of the creek. The cove area called Bell Lake and the river channel in front of Cherokee Creek are also prime places.

The waters near the dam also offer some good bass fishing. For example, the mouths of Hammock, Stoutamire and Blount Creeks are excellent spots to try. The mouth of the Oklawaha Creek where the channel enters the main Ochlockonee River channel also provides excellent bass fishing. The depths from 12 to 30 feet are full of trees, logs and other structure. In the late summer, bass are

One of the few large impoundments in the state, Lake Talquin is controlled with recreational interests receiving the top priority. A good quality map will help locate the better areas for bass fishing.

concentrated in the river channel bends area in front of the dam. They'll be in 15 to 25 foot of water when they are not schooling near or on the surface in the adjacent 12 foot deep flats.

LAKE DETAILS

Lake Talquin is located in the rolling hills of the Florida panhandle about 10 miles west of Tallahassee. It was named for the cities of Tallahassee and Quincy, and was formed in the late 1920's with completion of the Jackson Bluff Dam on the Ochlockonee River. The dam is located approximately 65 miles upstream from the Gulf of Mexico and approximately 20 miles west of Tallahassee.

The lake covers 10,200 acres and has a maximum depth of 50 feet near the dam. Talquin averages less than 15 feet in depth and is about 14 miles long. Even with those statistics, it is one of the largest impoundments in the state. Since the early 1970's, water levels have been relatively stable at an elevation of 68.6 feet above mean sea level. Planned drawdowns in 1983 and in 1990 reduced the volume of water and exposed about 60 percent of the bottom.

The lake gets its water from a dozen tributaries winding through the Tallahassee Hills region. They include: the Ochlockonee River, Little River, Double Creek, Hunter Creek, Rocky Comfort Creek, Harvey Creek, Polk Creek, Oklawaha Creek, Stoutamire Creek, Blount Creek, Mews Creek, Bear Creek and Hammock Creek. Water levels are maintained by the Jackson Bluff Dam. In 1957 a section of the earthen portion of the dam gave way due to heavy rains and high water. Repairs to the dam required slightly more than a year and water levels remained down during this period. Intentional drawdowns were conducted in 1972 and 1974 to perform other repairs to the dam.

Lake Talquin has about 52 miles of wooded shoreline which contributes to the fertile and tannic stained waters. Changes in types of vegetation occur each year, particularly before and after drawdowns and habitat restoration. The drawdown of Lake Talquin in 1983 exposed approximately 75% of the reservoir bottom. Accumulated organic muck underwent extensive drying and consolidation. Lush native and emergent aquatic vegetation began growing on some 1,500 acres of the exposed bottom in the spring of 1984, and by June extensive stands of vegetation had become established in the upper end of the reservoir and in tributary coves.

The refilling of Lake Talquin flooded all vegetation. Most of the aquatics survived and provided important largemouth bass nursery areas for several years. Additionally, several species of submersed aquatic vegetation, such as coontail and chara, became established in shallower of up to 6 feet. Emergent plant communities include: American lotus, or water lily, spatterdock or yellow pond lily, maidencane, peppergrass and smartweed. There are also four fish attractors on the lake which concentrate bass.

There are several free public launch areas on the lake. On the south shore at the east end of the lake off Highway 20 is the popular Coe's Landing. Further west, off Highway 20, is Williams Landing and Lewis Hall Landing. Limited parking is available at Ben Stoutamire Landing and Wainwright Landing, both also off Highway 20 near Stoutamire Creek on the west end of the lake. On the far west end of the lake about 1 1/2 miles north of Highway 20 is Blounts Landing.

On the north side of the east-west running reservoir there are three more public ramps. On the north shore off Highway 267 and at Hopkins Landing Road near Hammock Creek is a double ramp. About three miles south of Highway 267 on the east side of Hammock Creek is the Whip-Poor-Will Landing with very limited parking. At the west end of the lake off Highway 268 and High Bluff Road is the state-maintained High Bluff Landing. In addition to those access sites, there are a few additional resort/fish camp landing facilities around the lake.

For guide service, contact Mack Gainey, Gainey's Talquin Lodge, RT 7, Box 1607, Quincy, FL 32351 (904)627-3822, or Brad Sickinger & Belynda Shadowyn, Coe's Landing, (904)576-5590.

For information on this great area, contact the Tallahassee/Leon County Tourist Development Council, Leon County Courthouse, Tallahassee, FL 32301, (904)488-3990 or the Tallahassee Visitors Center, 200 W. College Ave., Tallahassee, FL 32302, phone (800)628-2866.

6

J-VILLE RIVERS AND CREEKS

I DUCKED THE overhanging limb as I set the hook with a side sweep of the rod. My hat was knocked from its perch into the boat as I continued to reel the fish toward me. I knew the bass was poorly hooked, and it jumped and spit the worm rig at me to prove the point. The slip sinker slapped the side of the boat.

My partner, who was battling a twin of the 14-inch largemouth that I had lost, laughed. Soon it was my turn, as he neglected the trolling motor and our boat was swept clockwise in an eddy. The fish seemed to know of my partner's predicament and swam around the electric motor's shaft.

"Need any help with that lunker," I cajoled, as he grasped at the trolling motor cable to pull it from the water.

The boat swirled clockwise while the small bass swam counter-clockwise, adding confusion to the scene. Overhanging tree limbs were again menacing as my partner finally gained a lip-lock on the fish.

Excellent and often overlooked bass fishing exists in the small creeks and rivers of Northeast Florida!

That happened to me on Thomas Creek several years ago, where such a scene is typical on the small creeks and streams of north Florida. In the process of landing a largemouth from a meandering stream, the boat is often swept into shoreline cover or turned by eddies. I have been high-beamed on submerged logs while chasing overlooked creek largemouth.

When fishing the narrow and twisting tributaries, where both banks can be easily cast from the same spot, such things add excitement to the experience. While a few waterways offer a bewildering maze of channels through treeless grasslands, most of

North Florida's small creeks 10 or 15 miles inland from the salty water along the Atlantic are bordered by forests. The often tannic acid-stained waters flow past an occasional waterfront cabin or home, but for the most part these areas are still primitive.

Lonely stretches of creeks are much more prevalent than a marina or boat ramp. In fact, the best access ramp to many of the tiny waterways may lie several miles downstream. It may even take a 20 to 40 minute run upstream to reach the best bass fishing on some waters. For larger bass boats, the triad of Mills, Thomas and Boggy Creeks which flow through the Nassau Wildlife Management Area normally requires such a run. Although a few ramps exist closer to the better fishing on those streams, the boater must either have a 4-wheel drive vehicle or be very familiar with the tidal effects in that area.

Regardless, suitable boat ramps are available on waters that subsequently provide access to some of the smaller creeks in North Florida. Many lie along U.S. 17 which runs in a north-south direction from the state line above Jacksonville past Lakes George and Crescent. Fishing pressure along that route is normally focused on the St. Johns River and not on the more primitive (and smaller) water courses. That means more bass for those who venture to the tiny creeks.

To access Thomas, Boggy or Mills, I've usually launched at a fish camp located on the Nassau River at the U.S 17 bridge. The channel upstream does a lot of twisting, but it's fairly easy to follow. There are a couple of shallow sandbars to navigate around on the way up, and once I reach Thomas, I'll normally continue upstream to a point about four to six miles above the "treeline." That's where the brackish marsh ends and the hard banks and timber begin on each side of the stream. The better bass fishing can be found along the upstream bends and wooded banks.

TIDEWATER BOUNTY

Friend Steve Hamman and I have fished Thomas, Boggy and Mills on numerous occasions, and we've never been skunked. Those waters seem to outproduce the larger rivers and natural lakes in North Florida. The majority of days spent casting worm and plug fare resulted in well over two limits of largemouth caught and released - one at a time. Bass there are not big - about the largest we caught was a shade over seven pounds. We have managed to catch one or more four pounders on most trips, though, and the 14 to 16 inchers are full of action.

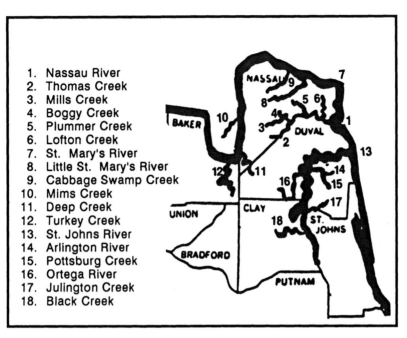

1. Nassau River
2. Thomas Creek
3. Mills Creek
4. Boggy Creek
5. Plummer Creek
6. Lofton Creek
7. St. Mary's River
8. Little St. Mary's River
9. Cabbage Swamp Creek
10. Mims Creek
11. Deep Creek
12. Turkey Creek
13. St. Johns River
14. Arlington River
15. Pottsburg Creek
16. Ortega River
17. Julington Creek
18. Black Creek

The creeks offer numerous bass among the brush and fallen trees that typically spill over from the banks. Like most of the small creeks in North Florida, the bass fishing there can be extremely hot or cold, depending upon the water level and other factors. I know that once you discover a concentration of bass, it is wise to stick with them.

Hamman and I once caught four bass as we drifted down a hundred-yard stretch along a wide outer bend on Thomas. We cranked up the outboard and motored up above the area of the first strike and drifted down again...and again...and again. Each pass, we caught and released four to six largemouth. None of those caught on subsequent passes had evidence of our previous hooking, so we figured that the concentration of bass there was tremendous.

The fish were actively feeding on a shelf below a shelf. The bank dropped quickly to three feet, tapered gently to four feet and then plunged to another shelf at eight feet. Plastic worms, rigged Texas-style, were pulled off the first flat to settle down on the deeper shelf, and that's where the bass concentration was located. We had released over two dozen bass when our day ended and we left the find.

FINDING AND FLOATING
THE SMALL FLOWAGES

Small creeks in the northern part of the state are often overlooked due to the publicity received by the St. Johns River and several "name" lakes which always seem to produce trophy bass - the kind great photos are made of! Some of the smaller tributaries also produce big bass, but seldom are the successful anglers willing to discuss their accomplishment. The tight-lipped fishermen are content with keeping the information and the fishing to themselves.

Such waters seldom require a large boat, although most can easily handle a 17-foot-long bass boat. Small aluminum john boats, one-man plastic boats, canoes and other tiny craft are comfortable on most of the creeks in that part of the state. On my first drift trip down the Ortega River, southwest of downtown Jacksonville, my partner and I fished comfortably from his 16 foot bass boat while a couple of friends squeezed into an 8-foot aluminum boat. It was quite a sight to see the two burly men in the tiny craft with seemingly only three or four inches of freeboard.

As on any water, anglers should keep safety in mind when employing boats of any size on these creeks. While some may be called "creeks," they are very wide in spots. Overhanging limbs and submerged trees are hazards along many. Docks along the few populated residential areas on most waters can also be obstructions worth watching for.

An electric trolling motor is a wise choice for most of the creek fishing in this part of the state. Currents are generally slow, unless heavily influenced by tidal movement or originating from a subterranean spring. The quiet motor will allow an angler to maintain a casting position while drifting downstream and to navigate around obstructions that may present themselves on the float.

IN THE BIG CITY

Jacksonville's Ortega River and tiny Pottsburg Creek have spots similar in nature and geography. Both dump into the north-flowing St. Johns River (Pottsburg through the Arlington River) 25 miles from its confluence with the Atlantic Ocean. The Ortega lies on the west side of the big river, while tiny Pottsburg Creek is on the east.

While a nice boat ramp lies just off Beach Boulevard, Pottsburg is seldom crowded during the week. Bass fishing along the wooded shores can be especially productive without the constant boat

The small creeks of North Florida offer some thrilling bass action and pretty scenery. Creeks, like Thomas, also offer quiet and peaceful fishing for a variety of fresh and saltwater species.

traffic that usually occurs on weekends. The creek is short, but the bass action is fortunately overlooked by most city dwellers.

The Ortega River also has excellent fishing for largemouth when the weekenders are not out in force. Deep holes in the bends harbor some exciting bass action. Fishing partner Ted Jordan and I once took a dozen bass from the wooded shoreline in less than three hours. The bass angling there is still a secret to many - we haven't been quick to pass the word to nearby souls.

Quite a few anglers do, however, know about the good bass action in Julington Creek just south of Mandarin. However, fishing is often tough, so fishermen don't spend as much time searching for concentrations of largemouth in those waters. The creek is beautiful, with huge fields of bonnets snuggling the banks and points where tributaries enter.

Such terrain, to the average angler, can be frustrating to fish. Hangups there, though, are evidence that an angler is putting his lure or bait in the right spots. Largemouth inhabit the pad beds, but they are not easy to reach at times. The successful angler on Julington is one that fishes it early or late in the day and effectively works the most weedless lures through the densest plant cover.

65

Largemouth of up to 17 pounds have been taken from the varying creek depths, but the average size is more like one and one-half pounds. Creek bass show a preference for large river shiners served on the edges of the deepest pads during the late winter, for shrimp offered under the docks during late spring, and artificials cast into the thick of things the rest of the year. Schools of Julington bass occasionally move into the bonnets and knock the stems around giving away their presence to observant anglers.

As on any flowage, knowing where to look is the key to finding bass. The quick drop off down to 10 or 12 feet with adjacent cover is ideal. A good LCD unit, like one of the Bottom Line Sidefinder sonars, is important on Julington, since much of the open water there is shallow, just three or four feet deep. Such water doesn't generally pose navigation problems, but the better concentrations of bass won't frequent such territory. Bass like to spend time in deeper waters most of the year.

SOUTH OF TOWN

Black Creek drains swamplands southwest of Jacksonville. Those deep waters flow into the St. Johns River 25 miles upriver from the city and just north of Green Cove Springs. The Ravines Resort can also be a landmark when boating from the host river. The property is located near Middleburg right on Black Creek about 7 or 8 miles from the St. Johns. Much of the better creek fishing is found within a mile or two of the resort.

The dark tannic stained water in the tributary gives the creek its name. Black Creek is the second deepest tributary in the state, according to the Army Corp of Engineers. A few holes 60 feet deep lie in spots along the scenic waterway and the average is around half of that. Deeper parts of the 30-mile-long tributary are found adjacent to the outside bends of the twisting creek. The shore-side waters typically drop off quickly, so productive baits there are often those that fall fast and run deep.

Many small tributaries run into Black Creek, and it is at those intersections where wise anglers concentrate. Bass and smaller forage fish also tend to congregate at those spots in the slowly-moving water. Fishing can be good up in the arms of those small creeks and in the deep-cut elbows of Black Creek. Pads and reeds along the tree-lined banks provide bass cover and enhance the opportunity for alligator sightings.

Artificial lures are most effective on the small meandering waterways of North Florida. On most of these waters, the boat traffic picks up on the weekends.

Since hardwoods line both shores, the drift down the creek is quiet and wind-protected. Several homes line this waterway and the fixed piers off many are great spots to catch a largemouth. Lures that can be worked in under the wooden canopies, such as Texas-rigged plastic worms, are ideal. They should be cast to the upstream side of the structures and allowed to drift into the potential bass habitat.

A convenient launch location is Black Creek Marina just off U.S. 17 about nine miles south of Jacksonville's I-295 bypass. Pollution from the mills near its origination at Palatka is not as bad as it was years ago, but the fishing can still be tough at times. Largemouth over 16 pounds have been taken from Black Creek, but the average size bass caught today is probably less than two.

For anglers seeking other quarry, a good striped bass fishery exists near the intersection of smaller tributaries along the creek and, specifically, at the junction of the creek's north and south Prongs. Stripers averaging 10 pounds are often taken at night.

67

NORTH IN NASSAU COUNTY

Another excellent North Florida largemouth and striper water along U.S. 17 is the Little St. Marys River. The creek-like tributary to the 100-mile long St. Marys River is usually overlooked by anglers more accustomed to big waters. In my experience, though, the smaller branch offers the most consistent fishing for bass. The narrow, winding waterway is deep and productive.

Creeks running into the sawgrass off the St. Marys River are narrow and tidal influenced. Many are deep, with bottoms 15 feet or more, and they normally contain largemouth. The tidal creeks of Nassau County offer seemingly endless miles of unexploited and productive waterways. The little ditch mouths often yield bass, particularly on a falling tide. Those with depth and some brush on the bottom are the most productive.

The St. Marys mahogany-stained waters offer good bass fishing for keeper-size fish, but few giants are taken. While a 13 pounder was taken a few years ago, most of the big fish there are six or seven pounds. Ramps at the highway 17 and U.S. highway 1 bridges allow full-size bass boats access to the St. Marys.

Most of the better fishing comes from above the U.S. highway 1 bridge. In fact, the upper 40 miles of the river is quite different than the large expanse closer to the ocean. A narrow waterway with fallen trees, log jams and sandbars offer a more picturesque venture. Deep outer bends with some type of wood structure yield the better largemouth here.

The Little St. Marys empties into the larger river west of the U.S. 17 bridge which spans the southern bank of the St. Marys. From the mouth of the small river upstream numerous largemouth bass await near dropoffs and sandbars. An irregular bottom makes for interesting angling for those wanting to drag a slip-sinker worm rig along the drops.

Several smaller creeks and tributaries lie along the Little St. Marys, and the mouths of them are always excellent spots from which to retrieve a crankbait or vibrating plug. Seldom will those have names, but they do have bass. A few shallow sloughs exist, and they are prime spots to check out early and late in the day. Very little activity exists along the picturesque waterway that is sheltered by brushy banks and fallen timber; that means better fishing.

Cabbage Swamp Creek, a mile or two west of the Little St. Marys, and Mims Creek, Deep Creek, and Green Creek, all several miles upstream, offer good bass fishing at times. Turkey Creek, another nearby St. Marys River tributary, has some water quality problems but does yield largemouth from the deeper outer bends.

Plummer and Lofton, both Nassau River tributaries, are excellent bass creeks in Nassau County. While access to some waters can be difficult, there's an easy-to-find ramp at the highway 17 bridge over the Nassau. Motor downstream to Lofton and upstream to several other tributaries. The dark waters of Lofton wind through pine and oak forests and marshes east of Yulee. Bass over 12 pounds have been taken from the creek by local fishermen. Outside bends and drops are most productive.

Most of the creek banks in the waters of Northeast Florida offer plenty of logs, stumps, tree tops and eddies behind such obstructions. Bass love such spots to ambush careless baitfish that may drift or swim by. They'll jump on current-swept baits like that morsel may be their last. Creek bass are hard strikers and fighters. They deserve respect.

Big crank baits, vibrating plugs and worms produce in most small waters. Smaller lures typically fool small bass, while big ones go for larger offerings. Artificials that are retrieved on or near the surface at the shoreline account for smaller fish, and bottom-bumping baits commonly attract the larger bass.

TACTICS, LURES & BAIT

The best of the Nassau tributaries for producing big bass may be Boggy Creek, according to Amelia Island fishing guide, Terry LaCoss. Fishing the vegetation such as lily pads, hydrilla, eel grass, and milfoil, in the upper reaches of the creek is often productive on bass up to 12 pounds. A purple with pink tail swimmin' worm tossed around heavy stands of weeds is effective during the high tide. LaCoss adds a small Colorado spinner in front of the plastic worm for maximum action.

On an outgoing tide, he recommends adding a 1/4 ounce slip sinker and fishing the worm rig in the deeper outer bends that have ledges just off the bank. LaCoss catches the bigger bass when the tidal waters have dropped, leaving much of the cover high and dry. Crankbaits fished around brush deadfalls and sandbars in feeder creeks are also productive.

When the baitfish are relegated to deeper waters, particularly during the last hour of the outgoing tide and the first hour of the incoming, the lunker bass seem to go on a feeding binge. The worm should be allowed to "roll" down ledges, while keeping the line as taunt as possible in the moving water. An excessive bend in the line creates strike-detection problems for those unfamiliar with tidewater fishing.

CONTACTS

Regardless of where one stops along Northeast Florida's Route 17, creek bass await. The angler's main problem then is to watch out overhanging limbs don't knock his hat off. The largemouth should take care of the thrills. For more information, contact Terry LaCoss at the Amelia Angler, Amelia Island Plantation, Amelia Island, FL 32034, or phone (904) 261-2870, or Peter Thliveros, the North Florida Bass Guides, 1306 S. Edgewood Ave., Jacksonville, FL 32205, or phone (904) 772-7927.

7

DOWN ON THE SUWANNEE RIVER

THE TRULY UNIQUE feature of the Suwannee River area is the battlin' bass that is endemic only to this watershed, the Suwannee bass. The fish grows to about 4 pounds, but it is packed into a powerful, short body capable of tearing up light tackle. A ten-inch Suwannee bass will weigh one and one-half pounds!

The last two all-tackle Suwannee bass records were caught in the Suwannee River. The previous record came from Dixie County, and the existing one was taken in March, 1985 by Gainesville angler, Ronnie Everett. He caught the 3-pound 14 1/4-ounce fish on a black spinner bait with green pork rind attached. Everett's state and world record Suwannee bass was pulled from the Suwannee River approximately one mile north of the Sun Springs ramp in Gilchrist County. The fish measured 16 5/8 inches in length and 15 1/8 inches in girth.

World record possibilities exist on this fabled bass water, and the numbers of largemouth will surprise most anglers!

My largest Suwannee bass, a 2-pound, 10-ounce fish from the Suwannee River, was caught on 12 pound test line. It was not a line class world record, however, like my smaller Suwannee bass taken from the tributary Santa Fe River. Knowing which rod has which pound-test line is vital to setting a record, as I learned during that trip to the Suwannee River.

I had launched my boat at Branford and was making a few casts near the ramp while waiting for a photographer from National Geographic Traveler to join me for an exploratory/photo trip on the river. My fifth cast with a crayfish-colored crankbait was jolted by a Suwannee bass. I carefully fought the fish to the boat and quickly realized it was my largest Suwannee ever. I emptied out my cooler, filled it with river water and the fish and headed for the local grocery about a block away.

In my boat's dry storage was the proper record application, so I obtained the required signatures and certified weight needed for submitting it to the IGFA. The 2-pound, 10-ounce Suwannee bass was a monster, but there was one problem when I got back home with the fish and application. I checked the Official Records booklet and found that the all-tackle record was caught on 12 pound test.

It was then that I realized that my fish wouldn't qualify in that line class. My mistake in using 12 pound test that day was a major one. That fish would have netted me another record in any other line category!

All rivers in the Suwannee River watershed contain Suwannee bass, in addition to the much larger largemouth. A fall float trip down the Suwannee offers springs, shoals, limestone banks, cypress trees and lush vegetation, plus bass.

As with any river trip, the entrance and exit locations should be planned in advance. Many Suwannee River anglers will embark at a downstream location, boat upstream to a selected spot and then drift back downstream a few miles to the convenient exit ramp. Bass boats with adequate power are perfect for such river trips.

Most of the enjoyable fishing floats through the often unspoiled Florida terrain along the Suwannee take about an hour per mile on the upper stretches. Plan on drifting six to eight miles during a day with plenty of stops for casting at the many likely looking spots.

Another way to float down the Suwannee is to park one vehicle downstream and drive another upstream to a launch point. The one-way float trip is ideal for small boats like cartoppers or canoes. You'll still need a small outboard for safety purposes. Take plenty of lures and fuel, you won't find any along the river.

UNKNOWN SPORT

The Suwannee bass was, and still is, a rare species that is only found in that watershed, and nearby in the Ochlockonee River. The lack of focus from fishermen is certainly not derived from the battle these bass species put up once hooked. I first tangled with one of the unknowns several years ago. It took me a while that day to figure out how to catch the fish, but once a productive pattern was established, I was able to tussle with several.

SUWANNEE RIVER

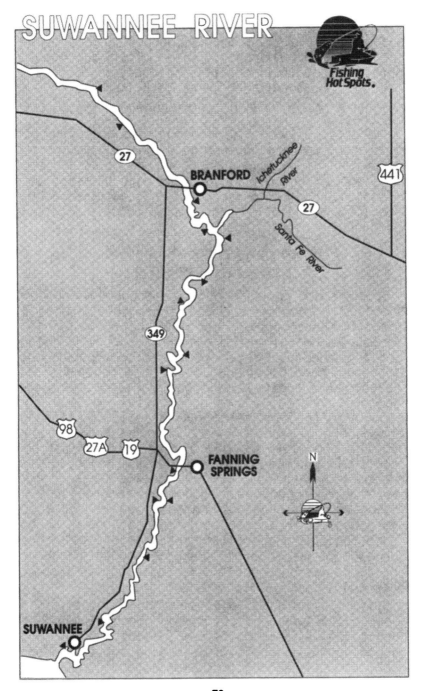

Fishing Hot Spots.

27

BRANFORD

Ichetucknee River

441

27

Santa Fe River

349

98

27A

19

FANNING
SPRINGS

N

SUWANNEE

My partner flipped a weedless jig and rubber grub combination against the steep limestone bank and let it sink slowly to the bottom. He had hardly started his retrieve when the lure stopped and his next move was a backward sweep of his rod. The 13-inch fish took out line against the drag momentarily. My friend hung on to the rod and finally boated the two-pound, one-ounce 'package' of fun.

The shoal areas were conducive to the Suwannee, while the vegetated, cypress-lined waters off the swift current usually held largemouth bass. We were after the rare species, but probably caught twice as many largemouth. Many trips since have been 'focused' on the rocky stretches of the Suwannee River and its legacy, the Suwannee bass. The fish fight two or three times their weight, and that's the attraction.

HABITS AND HABITAT OF
THE RARE SPECIES

This bass exists only in the limestone sinkhole region of north Florida and (minimally) in south Georgia, and is common in moderately swift, rocky stretches of rivers and spring runs. The Suwannee bass are range-limited by physiochemical and geological features of water quality. They prefer environmental stability, calcarenous spring waters of high pH and hardness, and a narrow water temperature range, which are probably found only to this region.

Due to the limited range, the Suwannee bass is considered a rare species by the Florida Game and Fresh Water Fish Commission. It inhabits shoals of exposed irregular limestone and springs that are prominent in the best stretches of the Suwannee River. Stomach analyses have shown that the rare bass love crayfish, which compose about 70 percent of their diet. Fresh water shrimp and fathead minnows also frequent the rocky stretches and are part of the Suwannee's intake.

The fish, which seldom exceed 12 inches in length, were first recognized as a species in 1949. They have a small mouth with upper jaw not extending behind the eye, brown sides with diamond-shaped blotches, and a bluish lower jaw.

Spawning first occurs when the water temperatures reach 64 to 68 degrees, which is usually in February or March. It may last on into late May.

The best way to explore the small creeks off the Suwannee River is to do so by small boat from a base of operations, such as a houseboat. This is ideal for a venture of several days.

SUWANNEE HOUSEBOATING

A Suwannee River cruise aboard a 44-foot houseboat is one unique way to sample the fishing on the beautiful waterway. On such an adventure, you can also enjoy boating, swimming, spring-hopping, and plain ol' relaxing.

A weekend houseboating vacation provides anglers with the freedom to pause and fish anywhere and anchor anywhere. Not having to worry about getting lost enhances the experience. Even better, you can take advantage of the late afternoon and early morning fishing without having to find your way in the dark.

A peaceful environment of scenic marshes, lagoons and creeks surround the Suwannee River. There are plenty of places to fish along its stretch between the Gulf and Branford, the 50-mile upriver limit of safe houseboat navigation. More than 20 clear-water springs, dozens of tributaries and miles and miles of wilderness exist along the Suwannee. East Pass is renown for producing redfish and other saltwater species. Largemouth are numerous around the many islands near the Gulf, in the freshwater canal systems and in the tributaries feeding the delta.

The floating "resorts," fully equipped with gas stove, oven, small refrigerator, cookware and kitchen utensils, linens and even a deck-mounted gas grill, are available at Miller's Marine in the village of Suwannee. The air conditioned houseboats sleep eight people comfortably. The fishing, serenity and tranquility of the majestic Suwannee River from the comforts of a houseboat cannot be duplicated.

75

TACTICS, LURES & BAIT

Small spinners, jigs and crankbaits fished along the areas of limestone outcropping are productive on the Suwannee bass. Anglers should cast the fare to all shoal areas, underwater dropoffs, fallen trees, and isolated rocks in the limestone based stretches. Learn to read the water from the way the current flows over the outcropping and establish an early pattern. You may just catch that trophy, albeit 12 inches long.

While largemouth are found in the slower waters around the lily pads an fallen brush, the swifter limestone areas harbor the Suwannee. Since most of the spunky bass are near the bottom and around either limestone rock outcropping or fallen trees, a bottom bumping retrieve is most successful. But a weedless, or "rockless", lure may be the only one that will last more than five casts. The bait should be near the bottom, and always moving.

When the lure stops, always assume that a fish is on the other end, otherwise a Suwannee bass may knock the rod and reel out of your hands. A fast retrieve is usually recommended to prevent hangups. To worry about the fast and chunky river bass not following or catching the lure is in vain.

Live bait works well on all bass species, but you'll probably need to anchor to effectively fish most places. Shiners and minnows are attention getters. Drift such baits in the eddies created by the limestone rock formations and fallen timber for maximum success. Particularly good spots for live-baiting are the line formed between tannic-stained water and the incoming clear water from a spring. Shiners and minnows are easy to keep alive in the waters that seldom get too warm. In fact, the areas near the springs are normally between 65 and 75 degrees.

Careful bait or lure selection and its presentation is a must, unless the angler wants to keep spending valuable float time tying on new baits. The most available forage throughout the region is the crayfish, and lures resembling one are preferred by local 'rivermen.' Brown and red colors are logical choices for most bottom bumping lures.

Largemouth often strike worm rigs fished in their preferred habitat of lily pads and submerged brush. An orange and brown jig with pork trailer, crayfish replicas in crank baits or plastic, orange/brown combo Snagless Sallys, as well as live crayfish, are effective producers.

RIVER DETAILS

The Suwannee River watershed drains 10,000 square miles of Florida/Georgia turf and contains over 50 springs. The watershed consists of the 265-mile-long Suwannee River, the Withlacoochee, the Santa Fe, and other shorter and smaller tributaries. The Okefenokee Swamp, just north of the Florida line, is the headwaters for the Suwannee and St. Marys Rivers. The scenic 630-square-mile tangle of vegetation and twisting tributaries provides excellent angling for medium-size bass in its numerous 'deep holes.' The bass fishing here, like on so many of the spring-influenced waters, is generally neglected.

From the small town of Fargo, GA, the Suwannee River stretches south for 100 miles. Twisting, quiet swamp water changes occasionally to white-water shoals above the Florida town of Branford, making its personality and bass fishing opportunities interesting. Its lower reaches are placid and picturesque with many limestone springs lying back from its banks. Excellent bass angling exists from the Gulf northward, and while spring water areas are incredibly clear, the better fishing is found in the tannic-acid stained water.

An excellent ramp exists at Branford at the U.S. 27 bridge over the Suwannee River. From it, you can access the Santa Fe River just a six-mile run downstream and most of the easily navigable water all the way to the Gulf. I'll normally use that ramp because it is usable under most water conditions.

One of the most detailed maps available on the area is found in the Florida Atlas & Gazetteer published by the DeLorme Mapping Company, P.O. Box 298, Freeport, Maine 04032. Another map is available from the Suwannee River Water Management District, White Springs, FL 32096. For more information on houseboat rental, contact Bill Miller, Suwannee Houseboats, P.O. Box 280, Suwannee, FL 32692, or phone (904) 542-7349.

77

8

SANTA FE'S UNIQUE BASSIN'

RETRIEVE OF THE diving plug had just begun when a fish smacked it and took off upstream. It wasn't a typical powerful run indicative of my quarry, the Suwannee bass. However, the two pound largemouth put up a respectable battle. Five casts later, my crayfish-colored crankbait fooled a three pound largemouth that put up a valiant fight in the currents of the Santa Fe River.

My wife Lilliam and I were tossing small lures, crankbaits and in-line spinners in search for the elusive Suwannee bass and a variety of species that might keep the slow hours moving. The beautiful river offers excellent angling for largemouth and for the tough-fighting Suwannee bass.

The best float fishing in the state offers a unique bass that will be everlasting in your memory!

Our search for the Suwannee bass ended when one stopped Lilliam's crankbait ten feet away from the rocky shoreline. The ten-inch fish fought like a heavyweight, but it was soon lifted aboard and quickly released. I cranked up the outboard and headed upstream to make another pass by the limestone outcropping.

The bow-mounted electric was lowered again for our float and I made a cast to the swift current beside the craggy shore. My lipped crankbait descended about four feet and was swept toward a jutting boulder when it bounced off it and came to an abrupt halt. I set back on the spinning rod as it buckled to the pressure of a strong fish.

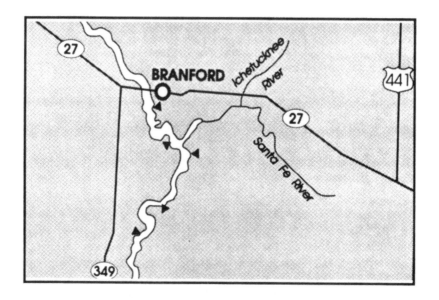

The fish didn't succeed in knocking the rod from my hands. I hung on in desperation, trying to gain control of the situation and of what I knew to be a sizable Suwannee bass. The spunky fish bullied itself to the brush we were drifting towards, and the line went limp.

Gone was the Suwannee bass that had won that battle, and I was left with my crankbait and its straightened hook. There was no way of telling how big that fish was. The tannic-stained waters of the Santa Fe hid that information, because I never really got the fish close to the boat.

And, like many of the clan when caught deep, that Suwannee bass didn't take to the air during battle. I was glad to still have the rod and reel, though, after such a strike. I know of two friends who have had their rod and reel knocked from their hands by memorable strike from Suwannee bass along the Santa Fe.

As the boat drifted another 100 yards downstream, I reshaped the hook and cast again to brush lying along a steep bank. My retrieve had only begun, when a fish smacked the plug and took off upstream. The power of the first fish wasn't there, and I soon pulled the fish into the boat.

I was mildly surprised to find the one and one-half pound black crappie dangling from the crayfish-hued crankbait. You never know what the Santa Fe might offer. Five or six casts later, I tied into a three pound largemouth. Lilliam and I finished out the short day with two Suwannee bass, six largemouth, one crappie and two huge bluegill.

We were tossing small lures, crankbaits and in-line spinners to the rocky structures along the Santa Fe in search of bass, and we found them. The productivity was typical, but there is more to a float trip down the Santa Fe than just the catch. The river is one of many spawned by springs in the limestone region of northern Florida, and it offers a vivid, unforgettable experience.

On my next cast, I hooked and carefully fought a bass on my 12-pound test line as it put up a battle beneath the surface. Finally, I saw it in the tannin-stained water as it neared the boat. The 14-inch Suwannee was chunky, weighing about two pounds, but steady pressure led her to a lip-lock at the gunwale. The bass was trophy-size for the species; few are caught much larger.

BIG SUWANNEE BASS

My largest Suwannee bass is a 2-pound, 10-ounce that was taken from the Suwannee River just six miles west of that area on the Santa Fe. I and two friends, however, caught three line-class world record Suwannee bass from the Santa Fe River. All weighed from 1 1/2 to 2 pounds. That may seem small for record fish, but the overall size of the Suwannee bass is smaller than bluegill or crappie. The small bass does, however, add immensely to the excitement of the Santa Fe River system.

The best way to set a record is to plan for one. The first time I decided to go after a Suwannee bass record, I looked through the "Official World Fresh Water Angling Records" booklet. I noted that most of the Suwannee bass line classes were vacant without a single qualifying fish. To catch a qualifying fish, one endemic to the north central part of Florida, I had to use the right tactics and also carefully plan for the event.

The booklet reveals information on how to establish a record catch. Line class divisions for each species were outlined and vary according to the maximum size of a particular species. For example, more divisions are set up for the flathead catfish than for a bluegill. Since the line classes for the Suwannee bass were open, I spooled five different reels with eligible line weights in two pound increments from 6 to 14 pound test. The same type of monofilament was used for consistency of breaking strength.

The rare bass doesn't grow much larger than a couple of pounds, and the all-tackle record at the time was only 3 1/2 pounds. I had caught specimens of the bass up to almost two pounds, so I was optimistic about establishing a record. According to creel census and electrofishing results from the Florida Game and Fresh Water Fish Commission, the chunky Suwannee bass is most abundant in the lower 30 miles of the Santa Fe.

WORLD RECORD TIMES

On my first record-hunting trip to the Suwannee watershed, a friend and I had about five hours of fishing. We selected crankbaits that were painted to resemble crayfish, the little bass' predominate forage. Based on the Commission reports, we chose to fish that 30 mile stretch of the river which joins the Suwannee just south of Branford, Florida.

It's interesting to note that the sport fishery of the lower Santa Fe River was also surveyed by the Commission for a one year period in the early 70's. Some 50,000 game fish were caught, of which 1.7 percent were Suwannee bass. Biologists calculate that it took 36 minutes on the average to catch one fish of some species, and 33 hours of fishing effort to land a Suwannee bass!

Naturally, those fishing for black bass improved on those statistics, but an angler specifically after the robust Suwannee can improve that significantly. Summer and fall catches are higher but the best time is probably in the late spring when the water recedes from the tree-lined banks.

Shoals of exposed irregular limestone are common on the Santa Fe, and those areas are where the Suwannee bass congregate. Elsewhere along the river, largemouth frequent lily pads, fallen trees and mud banks off the current. The river is influenced by several springs, including the Ichetucknee River, a crystal-clear run popular among snorkelers and innertube drifters. The Santa Fe, though, is tannic-stained over most of its 70-mile length.

I launched my boat about 7 a.m. that morning, and my partner and I began casting the crankbaits around all limestone outcroppings. We caught and released two largemouth bass before fooling a small Suwannee bass that wouldn't make one pound. The rocky shoals took their toll on our lures. With a strong current pushing us along, hangups were all too frequent.

My friend was the first to connect with a record fish. The 1 1/2 pound Suwannee grabbed the crankbait and was soon resting

This Suwannee bass weighed over 3 1/2 pounds and was a brief state record. This species seldom gains much length, but rather puts on additional weight through the girth. (Photo by Dewey Weaver, Game & Fish Commission).

in my live well. Fifteen minutes later, my crayfish imitation hooked another Suwannee, about the same size. Both fish were taken to the local grocery store and weighed on certified scales. Record forms were filled out, according to the instructions, and the line sample and applications mailed to the National Fresh Water Fishing Hall of Fame the next day.

About four weeks later, we were notified of our fishes' acceptance in the record books. Mine was short-lived, but my friend's mark lasted almost two years before it was broken. I took another friend to the Santa Fe River about three months after setting those records, and she set a line-class mark for the Suwannee bass with another that weighed 1-pound, 4-ounces. All three fish were caught on different weights of line.

HABITAT AND ENVIRONMENT

The Santa Fe has a unique character and an immense variety of animal, plant and bird life. It is typical of many spawned by springs in the limestone region of northern Florida. A journey down the Santa Fe reveals areas that are unspoiled and unpolluted. The picturesque river setting offers water birds such as blue herons and white ibis, and quiet river anglers may even see some otters. Some portions of the watershed have large concentrations of springs and sinks associated with the porous limestone formations.

Negotiating rapids and oft times tricky currents without bruising your hull may be difficult, but bouncing through occasional riffles can be exhilarating. Potential danger in boat navigation is always present during low water. Most of the float down the Santa Fe, however, is a serene experience through quiet pools beneath overhanging trees.

Cypress trees draped with Spanish moss guard the river banks. Their trunks reveal high water marks of years past. Water oaks and willows act as a canopy along narrow stretches of the river, while hollies, cedars and the glossy magnolia stretch skyward further back on dryer soil.

The Santa Fe is less clear than one of its major tributaries, the Ichetucknee, primarily due to the lesser influence of the springs along it. The Santa Fe is spawned by many smaller springs which have a lesser effect on water clarity and temperature. It is dependent in part to drainage from the swamps lying near its headwaters.

FLUCTUATIONS OF THE RIVER

The water level of the Santa Fe can fluctuate by 10 to 15 feet, depending on the rains in its own watershed and on those in southern Georgia along the Suwannee River basin. Average rainfall in the area between June and September is 7.5 inches. November, December and January are usually the driest months.

When waters are high, taking a boat through flooded cypress forests harboring beautiful crystal clear waters is a unique affair. The Santa Fe River is lined with lily pads, limestone outcropping and irregular bottoms often covered with eel grass and other aquatic vegetation. It also has its share of boat traffic, but most is limited to the weekends.

An angler can still rely on the quiet approach to catch bass along the Santa Fe. More times than not, he'll have to be satisfied with small bass, though. They may average one and one half pounds, and few exceed six pounds in these waters. The Santa Fe is just not known for producing heavy largemouth, but occasionally, it may yield one over ten pounds. To have a chance at a huge bass, a diligent angler should concentrate on fallen timber along the deep banks.

Floating the upper reaches of the Santa Fe from High Springs downstream eight to ten miles is often limited to the smaller craft. Riffles and shallow boulders are scattered along that section of the river. Larger boats and motors are better off staying in the lower 10 miles of the river. Navigation hazards are few and far between there, and there are just as many fish.

Many river bassmen - me included - grab a few tackle boxes stuffed with lures and head for the Santa Fe often. Once a pattern has been established on those waters (such as cuts off outer run bends over limestone rock) numerous areas can be found during the float trip.

That might take time, though. If you're like many other anglers, you'll be consumed often by the esthetic wonders of the Santa Fe. The river has a lot to offer any sportsman. The distractions are varied and most extremely interesting, but you should know of the options before you take the trip. Plan carefully, and you'll enjoy your adventure along the river.

TACTICS, LURES & BAIT

Heavy rains on the Santa Fe watershed generally result in less clarity than normal. Larger lures can be used when after members of the black bass family, and the angler can normally get away with slightly heavier line. A noisier retrieve may be dictated by such conditions, and shorter casts may be enough to entice a largemouth from its habitat.

Timing your casts is usually of concern when floating the Santa Fe since the boat and lure are constantly moving in a three to four-mile per hour current, and the waters may be dropping. The fish don't have the luxury of time to look over the offering and most successful presentations must take that into consideration.

Low water during a drought will result in a highly spring-influenced condition along some sections of the river and relatively clear water. The fish are correspondingly more cautious and difficult to trick on typical fare. Smaller lures for all species may be more productive then. A faster retrieve in areas of high clarity is also wise. The current will prevent a slow retrieve anyway.

A faster retrieve in areas of high clarity is also wise. The current will prevent a slow retrieve anyway. Retrieving the lure with rod tip placed well beneath the surface can be effective in catching those last-second strikes.

In general, the Santa Fe is most effectively fished by using the successful techniques experienced on other rivers. An injured minnow plug tossed under overhanging trees will catch the popular largemouth. The cast should be timed so that the lure drops upstream of the cover and drifts into it. A twitch or two above the structure and then a submerged retrieve out of the cover is usually effective.

85

Fallen and submerged trees and limbs are a favorite target of mine when fishing for largemouth on the Santa Fe. It's full of shoreline brush. Rising water can trigger bass into feeding binges and timing the fishing trip to those days is important. Once the water level has inundated the tree-lined banks, largemouth, in particular, may be difficult to locate.

Largemouth bass are the most common predator on the river and eight-inch long Texas-rigged worms fished in the heaviest concentrations of pads, bulrushes and pickerel weed are effective. Colors that resemble snakes work well in the waters normally stained dark by the tannic acid from cypress banks.

I'll drop the bait into each pocket along a shoreline bed of lily pads. Many bass can be located a few feet apart, and they can be caught. Often, it's possible to catch bass out of heavy cover right under the trolling motor. They'll hold fairly tight to the cover in a dense pad field.

RIVER DETAILS

The Santa Fe River runs for 26 miles from U.S. 41 near High Springs to its confluence with the Suwannee River at U.S. 129 near Branford, about an hour southeast of Tallahassee. The river joins the Suwannee 10 miles below Branford and is easily navigable for seven or eight miles upstream. Above that, travel depends on high water, as rapids and shoals are numerous. The average flow is approximately 1600 cubic feet per second, so the current will carry a boat swiftly along the ever-changing scenery.

Blue Springs, Ginnie Springs and Ichetucknee Springs are the three largest springs along the Santa Fe River, which is navigable by canoe from at least two miles north of High Springs on U.S. 41. Blue Springs is a deep pool with sandy bottom located in a private campground with picnic tables, grills, showers and restrooms. Swimming and snorkeling is permitted, and a boardwalk has been constructed from the spring to the river.

Ginnie Springs is a large pool with a short run to the Santa Fe. It has a privately-owned recreation facility which includes a dive shop, restrooms, showers, swimming, snorkeling and camping. A country store, boat ramp and canoe rentals add to the convenience of the area.

The Ichetucknee Springs group is located in the state park of the same name and includes nine named springs. There is no camping allowed at the state park, but private campgrounds are nearby. The Ichetucknee Spring spawns a crystal clear run six

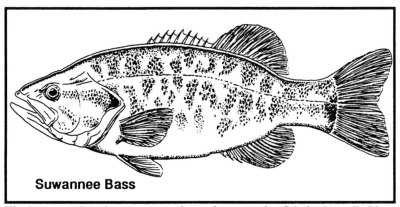

Suwannee Bass

The Suwannee Bass is an unexpected treat for many that fish the Santa Fe River. It is endemic to the limestone region of North Florida.

miles long where snorkeling, swimming and tubing are popular. The Ichetucknee River is also influenced by other springs, such as Cedar Head, Blue Hole, Roaring Spring, Singing Spring, Grassy Hole, Mill Pond and Coffee Springs.

Some of the other springs that lie along the Santa Fe include Devil's Eye, Dogwood, July, Naked, Rum Island, Lily and Poe. All lie upstream of S.R. 47 between the towns of High Springs and Ft. White. It's this area of the Santa Fe that clears the most during periods of low water. A crude boat launching ramp is available at Poe Springs approximately one half mile of S.R. 340

A few of the springs are on private property and allow no trespassing. Many of those spring runs are also shallow, swift and short. The public ones may not be navigable for the most part, but offer an interesting side trip by foot or backstroke.

LAUNCHING AND CAMPING

There are launching and picnic facilities at the U.S. 129 bridge between Bell and Branford, at Sandy Point, off S.R. 138 between Sandy Point and S.R. 47, off S.R. 138 near Blue Springs and at the S.R. 47 bridge between Ft. White and Trenton. Several other private ramps exist along the river for property owners in various communities. Low water and high water along the Santa Fe can make some of the entry points inaccessible at times. During normal water levels (and they are seldom at one level for very long), I sometimes use my property owners association ramp. I've had my cabin in the woods just off the Santa Fe for more than a dozen years now.

Campgrounds along the river include Blue Springs west of the town of High Springs where tent sites are available and the Ichetucknee River Run Campground. The latter is not on the river but offers groceries, propane, on-site rentals, tent sites and full hook-ups for RV's. Another camping spot on the Santa Fe River lies about 15 miles south of Lake City off U.S. 41/441 at O'Leno State Park. Here, the river disappears into a large, slowly swirling pool, flows underground and reappears three miles downstream. Obviously, you can boat through dry hardwood hammocks of oaks, magnolias, hickories and dogwoods.

O'Leno, with cypress stands mirroring themselves in still waters, is one of the finest nature parks in the state. Sinkholes surrounded by ferns, dense river swamp and rolling hills of longleaf pine support a wide range of animals. Nature trails, boardwalk swamp crossings and two separate campgrounds containing 65 sites with water and electrical hookups are available. Rustic cabins with a pavilion and dining hall may be reserved for groups. For more information, contact O'Leno State Park, Route 1, Box 307, High Springs, FL 32643.

9

HYDRILLA BASS ON LAKE SEMINOLE

SEVENTEEN POUND PLUS largemouth have been taken from Lake Seminole. One slightly over six is about the best I could catch in a few trips to the lake, but the trophies are there. Giant largemouth are usually caught in the spring when water conditions are right.

After a mild winter, largemouth bass move to bedding areas in mid-March, and then, in early April, a post-spawn feeding binge may occur. That's the bass activity most anglers are looking for. Cold fronts moving through this section of the panhandle in February and March will, however, delay such action considerably, according to guide Ted Kelly.

The Florida/Georgia impoundment's stump fields and weed-choked coves makes it one of the most productive, challenging bass lakes in the State.

Water temperatures ranging from 65 to 68 degrees seem to coincide with the spawning movement on Seminole. Water color, pH values, length of day, depth, currents, habitat, winds and bottom composition all affect the timing of the spawn. The tributaries, canals, sloughs and islands along the north side of the main-lake area are destinations for the largemouth bass spawning migration.

For those bassmen after a record fish, an exciting option does exist too. The Flint River above the lake (in Georgia) offers redeye bass, a smallmouth look-alike that is found only in a handful of waterways in the entire nation. The world record weighing 8 pounds, 3 ounces was caught in the Flint in October, 1977. The redeye fights like its cousin, the Suwannee bass, so it's a fish you shouldn't miss.

Anglers interested in the small redeye bass should focus their efforts on the river waters above Bainbridge. Boating can be hazardous in that area due to the flint rock shoals, so a johnboat is most suited for the trip. The best fishing, however, is when the waters are shallow, so the timing of the float is everything. During the summer months, waters are usually right. Use a worm or small crankbait to locate action here.

Because Lake Seminole is shared by Florida and Georgia, you may need two licenses. While there are waters where you can fish with one license, you can't fish all over Seminole with just one. A reciprocal license agreement between the two states exists on waters bounded on the west by Florida State Road 271; on the south by the dam; on the east by the line immediately east of the Chattahoochee Park and Booster Club, running northwest across the reservoir to the tip of land at the junction of the Flint and Chattahoochee rivers, west of Spring Creek; and on the north by the Herman Talmadge Bridge across the Chattahoochee River.

This popular bassin' area has a colorful history - Hernando de Soto crossed the Flint River near Bainbridge in the early 1500s. The town grew from an Indian trading post established in 1790 to a thriving community. A proud Indian nation, called Seminole, once lived on the lands now flooded by the Flint and Chattahoochee Rivers. Much of the forests were left standing, and as a result, careful navigation in Lake Seminole (Jim Woodruff Reservoir) is prudent. Submerged bass-holding structure, in the form of logs, can suddenly begin floating.

TACTICS, LURES & BAITS

I've used several effective tactics for catching Lake Seminole bass. Fishing the edges of the hydrilla and milfoil out in the lake is one of the most productive. Points and pockets of vegetation hold bass year around, particularly those near the spring holes and creeks around the lake. Often the aquatic plants define the intersection of two creeks, a prime spot for largemouth.

A vibrating plug, like the Rat-L-Trap, is particularly effective when worked in a "yo-yo" fashion over clean bottom runs. This pumping or flutter retrieve simulates that of a crippled shad trying to swim away from the bottom. Other lures that are effective when fished in this manner are the Little George tail-spinner and the Mann-O-Lure. Bass will strike these lures as they drop back toward the bottom. Keep a tight line and be ready to detect a soft strike.

The largemouth of Lake Seminole average two pounds, but many mid-size bass like this one exist in the dark-clear waters.

A plastic worm is also effective on spring largemouth when fished in the flats that vary from four or five feet deep. The large flats areas with numerous stumps and submerged trees are where bass congregate in February and March.

From March through October, the lake is one of the best topwater lakes in the southeastern U.S. Fishing the inside and outside edges of the vegetation with surface plugs, buzzbaits and floating plastic lures is very productive. Wood tail-spinner plugs and buzzbaits in white or chartreuse colors take their share of largemouth in the flats over the grassbeds near the dropoffs. The noise will bring bass to the surface from 8 to 10 feet down, and there's always a chance one will be a trophy. Just last year, a 14 1/2 pound Seminole largemouth was taken on a topwater plug.

In the summer months, employ the topwaters early and late in the day. Fishing the grasslines with tequila sunrise red shad plastic worms in waters 10 to 12 foot deep can be productive. Use a 3/16 weight on either a Texas rig or a Carolina rig. The area across from the dam at the rivers junction is a prime spot for worm action.

During the heat of the summer and the coldest part of winter, the mid-lake humps, sharp-tapering island points and old river channels in 18 to 20 feet of water hold bass. Plastic worms, such as Berkley Power Worms, and jigs should be inched along the submerged creek beds. Find structures and topography changes on sand and rock bottom in 10 to 20 feet of water for best action. The fishing is tough in July and August; the water temperature is high and the bass are inactive.

In September and October, employ a jigging spoon such as a Crippled Herring or Krocodile spoon along the bottom off the 25-foot deep river channel. Simply drop it down and jig it upward a maximum of two feet. You may be able to see the bass on the depth finder hanging off the side of a sandbar or dropoff.

In November and December, you may catch a few largemouth on top water buzzbaits, like the Lunker Lure, or on a stickbait like the Jerkin' Sam. Check out the shallow water. The lake usually turns over around the first of December; the warmer water at the bottom rises while the colder waters at the top falls. In January and February, the best fishing may be in Spring Creek if the temperature is extremely cold.

For the wade fisherman, there are plenty of shallow water spots. In some areas, you can wade-fish 1/2 mile from shore. Fly rodders using float tubes often have some exciting action around the numerous islands. For conventional tackle users, toss spinnerbaits around the vegetation on the flats.

WHERE TO LOOK

The Flint River near Bainbridge is a productive area for redeye bass. Fish the rocks, stumps and deep banks. The better largemouth action occurs in a variety of places along the Flint River arm of the lake. Wheaton Springs, for example, with waters along a stand of cypress trees varying from 3 to about 45 feet in the spring hole area is a good place to catch bass. Fourmile Creek is a good spot for largemouth. Bass also frequent the shallow water behind Camp Island, particularly the north end of the run around the island.

The Five Fingers area has waters from 3 to 8 feet deep that are productive spring largemouth spots. Butler Creek is also productive

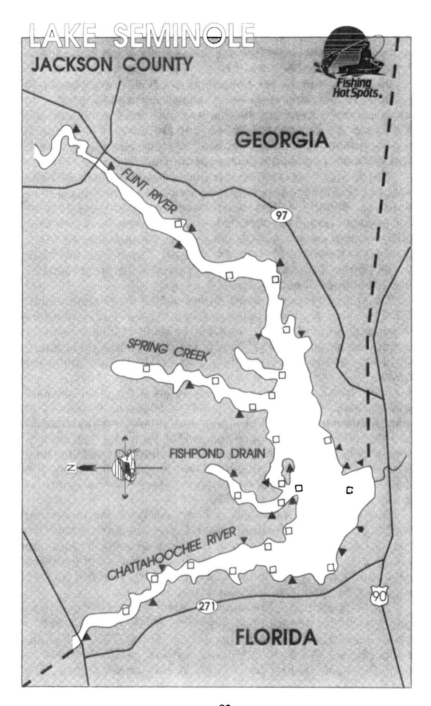

LAKE SEMINOLE
JACKSON COUNTY

GEORGIA

FLINT RIVER

97

SPRING CREEK

FISHPOND DRAIN

N

CHATTAHOOCHEE RIVER

271

90

FLORIDA

Fishing
Hot Spots.

for bass, as is the first slough south of it which offers hydrilla lying in about 7 or 8 feet of water. Big White Springs and Little White Springs both offer deep-water fishing for largemouth.

Sharp bends in the river where the depth may vary from 8 feet to about 25 feet deep at the river channel are usually good. The sandbars, which may move about in river currents from year to year are where the largemouth action can be found. Bass like to position themselves behind the sandbars and await forage. Use a depth finder to locate the best areas to fish.

The bass fishing is often excellent in the grassbeds off Goat Island and in the runoff water below Silver Lake when it is relatively clear. The Silver Lake Run is fed by seepage water through sandy soil from the small lake dam above. Once in a while, the water is milky but seldom is it muddy. While one 28 foot deep hole exists, most of the small run is relatively shallow. The area at the end of the No Wake Zone on Silver Lake Run can also be productive. Fish the stumps, logs and grass.

The grass edges along Spring Creek and the submerged stumps, hydrilla, lily pads, peppergrass and reeds in Carl's Pass are good largemouth spots. The Twin Islands area provides good largemouth fishing over about 10 acres. There is deep water close to the mouth of Carl's Pass making the fishing good in all but the coldest of winter.

The tip of Lewis Island is a crossing point for schooling bass chasing shad. The bass move around the island to the Mule Pen area. Between Rattlesnake Point and the Cannon Hole and adjacent to water depths over 20 feet are several sandbars that tend to concentrate largemouth. The Grassy Pond, Turkey Pond and Cypress Pond areas are all productive largemouth spots. The depth in the later averages about 12 to 15 feet in the flooded trees to less than 6 feet along the banks.

The big patches of lily pads in 6 foot depths in Ray's Lake and the peppergrass and hydrilla beds in Lewis Pond are productive bass areas. The mainland points with nearby deep water are usually good largemouth spots, as are the scattered hydrilla patches and flat off the river channel. The scattered grass and stumps of Saunder's Slough make it a good largemouth area.

The flats off the Chattahoochee River channel are excellent bass spots in the late spring and early summer. The most productive areas are near hydrilla in depths of 8 to 10 feet. The vegetation, which changes from year to year, harbors good quantities of threadfin shad. If the bass are not shallow, move closer to the channel. Sand ledges near the channel in 6 to 25 feet of water are also productive.

The grass islands on the west side of the Chattahoochee River offer depths of 3 feet with plenty of submerged logs. The man-made islands were formed when sand was pumped from the Chattahoochee channel. Most of the deltas off the river channel have numerous stumps that offer good spring bass fishing. The water clarity is usually ideal in April, and you can catch largemouth around the hydrilla and other grasses. By mid-summer, though, many shallower areas outside of the river channel are grown over with vegetation.

LAKE DETAILS

Lake Seminole, all 37,500 acres of it, lies in the Florida Panhandle (and Georgia), west of Tallahassee at the town of Chattahoochee. It was formed by damming the Chattahoochee and Flint Rivers below their confluence. The lake today has a maximum depth of 35 feet and an average depth of 9 feet. The river channels are actually maintained at 9 feet depths (and 100 feet wide) to allow for commercial river traffic.

Each of the two major arms, starting at the Jim Woodruff Dam, are approximately 25 miles in length, and the lake spreads over 58 square miles. There are approximately 500 miles of shoreline and over 250 islands scattered all over the lake. The maintained channel extends to Columbus, Georgia, on the Chattahoochee River and Bainbridge, Georgia, on the Flint River.

The Lock and Dam was constructed in 1947 as a multi-purpose project for navigation, hydroelectric power production and related water uses. The lock was opened to navigation in 1954 and power generation began in 1957. The Chattahoochee River Basin borders three states: Alabama, Florida and Georgia. The Flint River Basin and Spring Creek Basin (a lesser tributary) are entirely in Georgia. The Florida portion of the Chattahoochee River arm consists of the lower 9 miles and a surface area of approximately 18 square miles.

Three feeder streams with a drainage area of 17,150 square miles supply the lake's water. On the eastern side, the Flint River flows approximately 250 miles. On the northeast side of the lake is Spring Creek, a much shorter, clear water tributary. The western half of the lake is supplied by the Chattahoochee River which flows over approximately 300 miles.

Seven or eight major springs are located in the tributary runs flooded by the lake, and another 16 or more small springs are known to guides working these waters regularly. Five of the major springs, however, are being considered for closing for up to five years by the Georgia Department of Natural Resources. It would be wise to check existing regulations before fishing any springs here.

There are numerous back-water sloughs, small bays and ponds hidden at the ends of narrow, winding creeks in the lake. A dam exists on the Flint River above the lake at Albany, and there are two locks on the Chattahoochee River between the lake and Columbus, Georgia. The terrain around the lake varies from flat on the north sections to gently rolling hills and bluffs on the southeast portion of the lake. There are many associated sloughs and minor tributary branches along the north side of the main lake.

There are approximately 4,000 acres of vegetation on Lake Seminole with hydrilla being the primary submerged variety. Hydrilla beds flank much of the shoreline and inundate areas of standing timber. It, along with Eurasian milfoil, is normally found in the lower Spring Creek and lower Fish Pond Drain areas. Peppergrass, coontail, and giant cut grass are aquatic plants which grow on Seminole. Aquatic plant control programs have helped control hydrilla and other vegetation on the lake.

Contact Jim Woodruff Dam Resource Manager, Lake Seminole, U.S. Army Corps of Engineers, P.O. Box 96, Chattahoochee, FL 32324, phone (912) 662-2001. For information on the varying regulations on this impoundment, contact Georgia Dept. of Natural Resources, 270 Washington St. SW, Atlanta, GA 30334 and Florida Game and Fresh Water Fish Commission, 620 S. Meridian St., Tallahassee, FL 32399.

LAUNCH AND GUIDES

There are 30 public launch sites on this massive lake. Here's a rundown: on the west side of the lake off Highway 90 is the Sneads Park ramp. On the west side of the lake off Highway 271 is the 682-acre Three Rivers State Park. On the Chattahoochee River Arm of the lake on the east side of Highway 271 is a Jackson County Public Ramp. Other, more popular ramps off Highway 271 are at the Apalachee Game Management Area and at Paramore Landing Park.

Several other ramps are available on the Chattahoochee River Arm of the lake. On the west side, off Highway 271 is the Buena

Submerged brush and trees in the flats adjacent to a river or creek channel is a top action spot for Seminole's largemouth.

Vista Access Area. On the northwest end of the lake off Highway 91 is Neal's Landing Public Use Area. On the east side off Highway 221 in Georgia are two: the Desser Access Area, and the Fairchild's Park Access Area. On the western end of Highway 253 is the Butler's Ferry Landing.

On the north side of the lake off Highway 39 is the Cummings Landing Public Use Area, and off Highway 374 is the Ray's Lake Access Area. On the north side of the lake off Highway 253 is the Seminole State Park, and directly off Highway 374 is the Sealey Point Access Area. On the north side of the lake directly off Highway 374 is the Cypress Pond Access Area, and directly off Highway 253 is the Spring Creek Park Access Area. On the Spring Creek Arm off Highway 253 are Reynoldsville Park, the Decatur Lake No. 2 Access Area and the Ralph King Boat Landing.

There are numerous ramps on the Flint River Arm of the lake also. Off Ten Mile Still Road is the Ten Mile Still Landing and Hale's Landing Park Access Area, and off Highway 311 north of Bainbridge, Georgia is Big Slough Park. Off Highway 84 in Bainbridge is the popular Bainbridge Municipal Park, and on the west side of Highway 97 adjacent to the Bainbridge By-Pass is the

Bainbridge Park and Earl May Boat Basin. On the east side off Highway 97 are the Horseshoe Bend Park, the Faceville Landing Access Area and Hutchinson's Ferry Landing.

On the south side of the lake off Booster Club Road is the River Junction Access Area and off Highway 90 is the Chattahoochee Park and Booster Club Landing. On the south side of the lake off Highway 90 just north of the town of Chattahoochee is another paved launching ramp at the East Bank Campground and Public Use Area.

Several Seminole guides are productive. Contact Lunker Lodge Guide Service, Jack Wingate's Lunker Lodge, Rt. 1, Box 3311, Bainbridge, GA 31717, phone (912) 246-0658; Ted Kelly Professional Guide Service, phone (912) 246-0498; Leon Weaver's Lake Seminole Guide Service, Route 1, Box 2481, Bainbridge, GA 31717, phone (912) 246-7378; and Angling Innovations Guide Service, Paul Tyre, 3030 Lakeshore Dr., Tallahassee, FL 32312, phone (904) 385-2082.

10

THE STATE'S BEST HYBRID ACTION

IT WAS A COVER-UP. The red mud flowing swiftly past our boat hid any chance we might have had to identify the source of Johnny Chapman's doubled-over bass rod. The Woodland, Georgia, venison processor had the battle of the day fighting the current of the swollen Flint River with a powerful, yet inadequate 24-volt trolling motor while trying to gain control of a fish much larger than the four five- to seven-pound hybrids we had just caught.

I peered into the turbulent waters for a glimpse of Chapman's adversary while the burly fisherman put pressure on the fish and gained line. The final 30 feet of the 20-pound Trilene was almost on the spool when the giant fish ran off against the drag once again.

Lake Seminole offers hybrid striped bass action that you cannot forget!

"It's either a big catfish or a striper," Chapman predicted. "Look at that boil!"

The water, stained red from some 10 inches of rain in the watershed during the past week, erupted at the surface two more times before we got a glimpse at the fish. He was right. The powerful striped bass that had helped the current push our boat about a mile downstream was later weighed just shy of 20 pounds.

A crankbait had fooled the big Lake Seminole striper, despite the terrible water conditions. Chapman and I also had taken the other fish on a combination of Poe's deep-running crankbaits and Rat-L-Traps. We returned to a rocky stretch of the river and continued to produce fish on the lures. Five more hybrid stripers and a couple of three-pound white bass all fell for our lure selection.

Lake Seminole can give up such a variety on most any given day, but conditions are usually better to achieve it in the cooler months, according to Chapman. He has caught numerous stripers, hybrids and white bass in the lake over several years. In fact, he claims to have spots where he can catch some of the fish on any given day. After experiencing our success that uninviting day, I tend to believe the man.

The base of our eventful striper expedition was a rustic fishing camp near Bainbridge, Georgia. Jack Wingate, owner of the Lunker Lodge, has lived on Lake Seminole for more than 33 years and is a valuable source of additional striper/hybrid information. Being on the water almost daily has provided him with in-depth knowledge of the activities of the stripers and hybrids that roam the lake.

One only has to look at the walls of Wingate's restaurant and country store to realize the potential of the fishery. The walls are papered with photos and stringers of giant fish. The largest mounted striper weighed 43 pounds and the biggest wallboard hybrid was 18 pounds, 14 ounces, a lake record.

TACTICS, LURES & BAIT

Wingate often fishes for the hybrids and stripers that cruise the lake, so he knows the best tactics. To locate the better hybrid locations, he'll peer at his depth finder for dropoffs and grass bed edges. Those structures that make a sharp point in the lake are excellent places to find the fish.

"The optimal spots have adjacent deep water where the predators will congregate," Wingate says. "They will wait there for the shad to come around the point. Some of the better areas are Fort Scott, the Hutchinson Ferry Bank, Coot's Landing and Stone's Landing. The latter two are especially good locations to find hybrids, stripers and even white bass.

In the winter, the hybrid and striper fishing on Lake Seminole is often related to the tributaries or to the various spring holes, if open to fishing. The springs bubble right out of the bottom, and the hybrids and stripers lie near the bottom in 60 feet of water. The state of Georgia is, however, considering closing some of the primary springs to fishing, according to Wingate.

Most of the roving fish will stay in the deep creek channels and surface-feeding striper action will be minimal in January, according to guide Ted Kelly. If the water color is right, not muddy, that's the

Hybrid stripers grow fast, and they are probably the strongest fresh water fish for their size. The author shows a couple of Lake Seminole hybrids.

month when an angler has a chance at the biggest stripers. He and a guide party once caught three large stripers, or "rock fish" as he calls them. They weighed 24, 32 and 36 pounds.

"You can catch a lot of big hybrids too, 10, 12 and 14 pounders," Kelly says. "We caught 14 one day that weighed 104 pounds. It's nothing unusual to catch 10 in a day that may weigh 12 pounds each."

Kelly has fished for Seminole hybrids over many springs. On one day, Kelly and his party of two anglers caught (and released many) 42 hybrids that weighed 10 to 14 pounds each! One of the men fishing 20 pound test line lost six Rat-L-Traps before loosening his reel's drag.

In the winter, Kelly will concentrate on areas just off the spring holes and on the deeper waters near the dam. Some hybrids will start schooling in the late winter and gulls may find the action for you, according to the guide. Stripers can be caught right in front of the dam with live bait, such as threadfin shad, wild shiners or bluegills. Kelly also uses a jigging spoon on occasion.

The striper and hybrid action has been rejuvenated in the past few years thanks to an influx of hydrilla. While the growth of the plant in the summer makes fishing more difficult, it provides excellent habitat for forage and predator alike. In the winter, the hydrilla dies back, and the fish are easier to locate and catch. The most fertile weed beds can then be found by searching the expansive waters for coot, according to Wingate. Thousands of the ducks feed on the submergent vegetation during winter.

MORE STRATEGIES THAT WORK

In the summer, jump fishing picks up on Lake Seminole near the dam. A mix of small stripers, sunshines and white bass are commonly taken. For jump fishing the schools that are feeding on shad, minnow plugs or jerkbaits and topwater lures are best. Either one of the twosome with a small white jig rigged as a trailer one foot behind the plug can be especially effective. Once they sound in the depths, jigging spoons are a good choice.

Stealthy angling in the deep, cool spring holes scattered around the lake from June through August is smart if after a trophy striper. The big fish can hole up over the summer in the relatively-constant 74 degree water flowing from over two dozen springs in the lake and its tributaries. Live, river-caught threadfin shad, 5-inches long, are the deadliest summer bait for trophy-size stripers when found in concentrations at the thermal refuges. Small bluegill, eels and larger gizzard shad are also good live baits to fish in the spring holes.

Sunshines and stripers both travel in schools and spend much of their time in open water. Trolling with eyes on the sonar unit is the most effective way to locate these schools. In the fall, a vigilant eye should be kept on the surface to detect schooling fish or birds feeding on small baitfish. Largemouth, stripers and sunshine bass may be feeding on the threadfin shad. Top water plugs, like Griffin's Jerkin' Sam, and jerkbaits, like the Bomber Long A, are still productive for jump-fishing. Action may remain hot through December, depending on the weather.

Sunshine bass are taken year-round, but they prefer to school and feed vigorously during the cooler months of the year. They will take live bait, such as minnows or saltwater shrimp, quite readily, as well as strike small spinners, shad-resembling plugs and jigs. Jig size selection on lake waters should be based on the size of the forage on which the stripers are feeding and on the depth being fished.

Fishing with bait minnows at night with a bright light as a fish attractor is popular and productive for striped bass. In fact, some of the best stringers of stripers caught during the winter are taken at night. The fish are more active then. Flowing waters attract stripers, and fishing such areas frequently results in fine catches.

The prime time to locate and catch stripers in the lake is at the height of the spawning migration during the first 10 to 12 weeks of the year. Fishing the points in the rivers become very productive from January through March. For maximum success, locate and fish those that are prominent enough to force the swift current to eddy or swirl behind it.

Most anglers will cast from boats positioned mid-stream toward shore, into the point. Those with weak trolling motors that won't hold the boat in the currents may have to make several passes by the point. Effective lures are fast-moving crankbaits, tail-spinners and Rat-L-Traps. Heavier baits are tossed toward the points with sharper dropoffs and brought along the bottom. The most productive retrieve is to work the bait down across the point and through the eddy.

ACTION BELOW THE DAM

When the lake fishing suffers from cold fronts, the Apalachicola River spillway below Jim Woodruff Lock and Dam is a hotbed of fishing activity. That's where large schools of white bass, sunshines and stripers congregate. Much of the early spring fishing is off a catwalk where successful anglers use a 3 ounce lead weight, wire leader and live bait, such as eels, shiners or shad.

Both bank and boat fishing affords good opportunity almost year around, though, for quality-size fish. Bank fishermen can fish from the dam's east-bank catwalk, reaching it by taking the river road off Highway 90 west of Chattahoochee. Massive schools of shad fight the turbulence and thundering waters beneath the open concrete spillways. Gulls swoop down from above the turbine-generated mist, as the sport fish work on the shad from below.

Boat anglers may be at a slight disadvantage because a fixed buoy line keeps them 800 feet away from the dam. Anchoring in the headwaters of the Apalachicola River, below the confusion and tossing heavy spoons into the river's main run is, however, very effective. Another popular artificial for striped bass below the Lake Seminole dam is the 1/2 to 1 ounce white or yellow jig. In the tailrace area, fishermen adapt to swift current conditions by tossing jigs weighing 3/4 to 1 1/2 ounces that will sink into 15 foot depths quickly. Striper anglers normally employ heavy bait casting or spinning tackle with lines testing 20 to 30 pounds.

Stripers are powerful fish whether in or out of a current. A quality line and good tackle are necessary to catch one, and a light drag is often required to absorb the jarring strike. A giant striper will make an initial surge, and then the drag can be slightly tightened for better control. One of the best areas for catching a giant hybrid or striper is the first 3 or 4 miles below the dam on the Apalachicola River.

WHERE TO LOOK

During the spring, five and six pound hybrids can be caught in the numerous deep-water springs that exist on the Florida/Georgia border lake. Most of the roving fish will stay in the deep creek channels then. At this time of year, hybrids and stripers lie in the springs near the bottom in 60 feet of water.

The best areas to chase winter stripers on Lake Seminole are at the mouth of Spring Creek Run, the Indian Mound area at the confluence of the Flint and Chattahoochee rivers, and along the Flint River above Sanborn Creek. During April and May, stripers may be found rambling around the lake.

There are many other areas on the lake in which to find hybrids (sunshine bass), white bass or stripers. On the Flint River Arm, white bass and small hybrid striped bass school at the mouth of Fourmile Creek. White bass, stripers and hybrid stripers often concentrate at the rock pile near the mouth of Dry Creek. Another rock pile that draws all three species is located just below Sanborn Creek. Big White Springs and Little White Springs offer deep-water fishing for striped bass. Fish in 18 to 20 feet of water on changes in topography for best action.

Whidden Springs, with a bottom varying from 30 to 45 feet, is one of the deepest in the lake and is an excellent spot for stripers. Sealey Springs is also productive for striper and hybrid striper fishermen. During the latter part of April, and then on though June when water temperatures warm, the stripers and hybrids move into or near to the springs.

Spring Creek flows into the Flint River at this point, and striper and hybrids move through this area on their way up and down the creek. Hybrids and stripers gather in the depths, down to 20 feet, and enjoy the cool water coming from Spring Creek.

In the winter, the fish tend to school along the channel dropoff, the adjacent points and the humps in deeper water. The Indian Mound area yields hybrids, stripers and white bass almost year around. Schools of shad pass back and forth along the channel which varies between 10 and 20 feet.

Johnny Chapman favors crankbaits for Seminole hybrid action that he finds on a regular basis. To locate striper and hybrid action in the winter, he searches for rockpiles and bars in the tributaries.

LAKE STRIPERS

Lake Seminole offers the best striper and sunshine bass fishing in Northwest Florida. Gulf stripers were landlocked when the mile-long Jim Woodruff Dam was constructed in 1957. They adapted well to the fresh waters and today spawn and grow to over 70 pounds in the reservoir, according to federal fishery biologists. Stripers exceeding 60 pounds have been taken and released by fishery personnel and sunshines over 19 have been caught in the tailrace below the hydroelectric dam. The stripers have migrated up from the Gulf to spawn at the base of the dam.

The average striper in the lake will weigh 10 or 12 pounds and the average sunshine bass around 5 or 6 pounds. Florida state records for both were caught on Lake Seminole, a 38 pound, 9 ounce striper and a 16 pound, 5 ounce sunshine. The lake record striper caught on the Georgia side is several pounds heavier.

Stripers often move around on the lake. When the water temperatures reach 48 degrees, they move from the main body of Seminole north toward locks that regulate the flows of the Flint and Chattahoochee rivers. Once they move through the locks, the stripers continue upstream to drop their eggs. They migrate long distances up the rivers in waves, not all at the same time.

During the spring, as waters warm, the stripers will move back down river. As summer drives water temperatures higher, they move into the cooler waters of springs in the lake. The stripers remain there, foraging little until the ambient lake temperatures fall, and they again move out into the lower extremities of the reservoir in the autumn and early winter months, feeding ravenously.

Currently, stripers and sunshine bass are both being stocked in Lake Seminole. Over one million sunshine bass fingerlings and juveniles have been stocked in the past three years, and striped bass fingerlings have been stocked at even a higher rate. Because striped bass and hybrid populations are maintained by hatchery stocking and research has shown low survival for catch-and-release fish, small minimum-size limits are deemed inappropriate by the Florida Game and Fresh Water Fish Commission.

The current Florida regulation governing these fishes provides for a 20 fish aggregate bag limit (striped bass, sunshine bass and/or white bass in combination) with no more that 6 specimens over 25 inches in length and no more than 6 being sunshine bass. This allows a generous angler harvest of smaller fish while providing limited protection for trophy-size fish. The current Georgia limit for the striped bass, white bass and hybrid striper is 15 in aggregate with only two exceeding 22 inches in length.

LAKE DETAILS

There are approximately 12,000 acres of standing timber, stump fields and other mid-lake structures, as well as miles of hard-bottom flats in Lake Seminole. While the lake was cleared along the navigational channels, the timber was left standing elsewhere. The water clarity varies from very clear in areas like Fish Pond Drain and Spring Creek to translucent green in the main lake to sometimes a reddish mud complexion in the major rivers after watershed rains. Murkier water can often be found on the Georgia side of the upper half of the Chattahoochee River arm and in most Flint River sloughs.

See the previous chapter for complete details on Lake Seminole. For more information on the striper and hybrid fishing opportunities, contact Ted Kelly or Jack Wingate at Wingate's Lunker Lodge, Rt. 1, Box 815, Bainbridge, GA 31717, or phone 912-246-0658. Chapman can be contacted through Richard Saye Guide Service, at 206 Sturbridge Drive, LaGrange, GA 30240 or phone (404)884-1024.

For information on the varying regulations on this impoundment contact the Jim Woodruff Dam Resource Manager on Lake Seminole, the U.S. Army Corps of Engineers, the Georgia Dept. of Natural Resources or the Florida Game and Fresh Water Fish Commission.

11

BASS WITH A
SOUTHERN ACCENT

YOU DON'T SOON forget a day like my first one in the state in 1968. I was launching a small aluminum rental boat from Red and Sam's Fish Camp on Lake Jackson about 8:30 a.m. and returned just two hours later with the best of memories. A friend from Alabama and I shared the boat and the exciting catch.

We were fishless after 30 minutes, but that quickly changed at 9 a.m. when the lunker bass of Jackson broke loose. In about 40 casts, we had strung 7 bass that later weighed 68 pounds. They ranged from 7 to 11 1/2 pounds! It was like a school of giant bass had moved in on Brill Point where we were anchored. Our 10-inch Lake Jackson worms were gobbled up by the lunkers eager for battle.

Lake Jackson was this country's first renown giant bass producer. It and the other area lakes still offer good bassin'!

I'll never forget that brief episode, since it made me quickly decide to spend the rest of my days in the sunshine state chasing such fish. Times have changed, though. In those days, I, along with everyone else, kept the big fish to show off. They were for hanging on a long stringer. The state fisheries biologists, after all, had repeatedly said that we couldn't fish out a lake. Fishing pressure alone just couldn't diminish the quality of such a fishery.

Hogwash! The super Lake Jackson fishery was destroyed within a couple of years. Today, with proper emphasis on catch-and-release fishing, it is back, but not as it once was. Still, it can and does provide good bass fishing.

This ancient photo from 1968 shows the 7-bass stringer that the author and a friend caught in just one hour on Lake Jackson. Unfortunately, "catch-and-release" was not in the vocabulary of anglers back then. The author, a strong advocate now for over 15 years, has released hundreds of bass this size since then.

I won't forget that early trip, or one taken at night on the connecting Lake Carr in the early 1980's that resulted in a 10 1/2 pounder. I may someday forget about my last trip there this year when guide Paul Tyre and Mike Fine' of Berkley found some of the bass to be cooperative. We (Paul caught most of them) caught and released about a dozen one morning. None were over two pounds.

Such a day is now typical, and that's not too bad. With nearby Tallahassee booming, fishing pressure resulting from a "big bass explosion" like the one in the late 1960's would quickly wipe it out again.

The 4,000-acre lake alongside highway 27 on the northern outskirts of the capital city still yields some giant fish, but not like that June day in 1968. Three bass over 14 pounds each came in that morning at about 10:30 a.m., and they made our stringer look small. The record bass from the lake, caught on a topwater lure back in the hey days of March 1967, weighed 18 1/2 pounds. Today, an 11 1/2 or 12 pounder would grab some deserved attention.

DEPTH AND LURE VARIATIONS

Jackson is a relatively shallow lake with few holes over 10 feet deep. The "Porter Hole", also called "Porter Sink," is about 17 feet deep and the "lime sink" is 25 feet deep at normal water levels. Brill Point and Rollins Point are two well known bass hangouts. Pads, grass and hydrilla are abundant in these waters, which can vary from about 3,000 acres to over 7,000 depending on the water

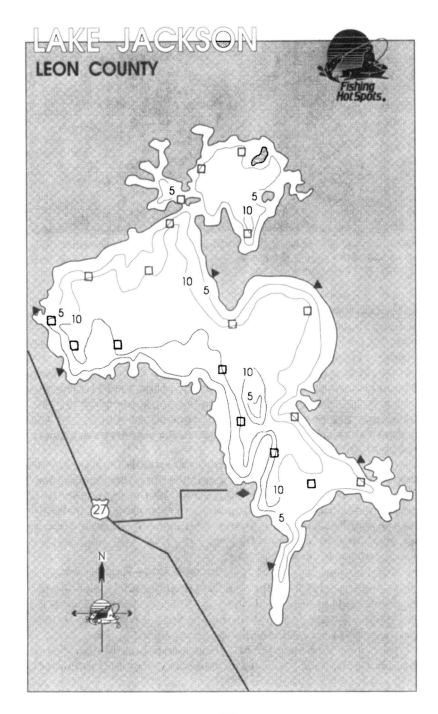

Today the grass beds of Lake Jackson still hold bass thanks to conservation efforts on the part of the Florida Game and Fresh Water Fish Commission and, more significantly, on the part of the modern day angler.

level. There is no major creek tributary to keep the water level up. In fact, about every 25 years, the lake experiences a "natural drawdown". A sinkhole in the bottom sees that, and an area drought may even hasten the time frame.

The drying up and airing out in the long run rejuvenates the relatively clear-water lake. With the water gone, the flat turns into a sea of grass. The two major arms on the southern end of the lake, Megginnis and Ford's, provide the brunt of the runoff from the limited watershed area. Thus, rainfall on the lake basin is the main source of water.

On Lake Jackson, plastic worms are certainly in favor for the largemouth. Guide Tyre likes to toss odd colors like "bubblegum" and yellow, and they work! Berkley Power Worms in pumpkinseed do also, as we found out on our recent trip with Tyre. The pads that hug the shallows and shore provide exciting action early and late in the day. In-line spinners, like the Snagless Sally, and floating plastic worms are effective there.

What else works on Jackson? Johnson Silver Spoons, vibrating plugs, like the Rat-L-Trap, and minnow-type plugs, such as the Baltic Minnow or Jointed Rebel, are often effective. After dark, the black Arbogast Musky Jitterbug is hard to top. And, shiners always account for some trophies in the colder months.

For some mind-boggling nighttime pad action, though, boat to the north end of Lake Jackson through a six foot culvert connecting to the other side, called Lake Carr.

112

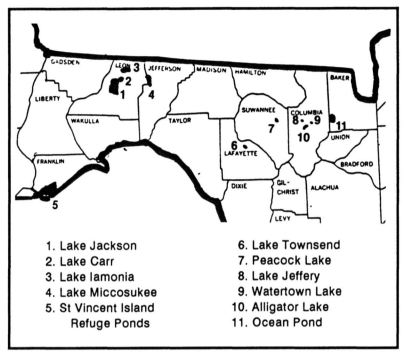

1. Lake Jackson
2. Lake Carr
3. Lake Iamonia
4. Lake Miccosukee
5. St Vincent Island
   Refuge Ponds
6. Lake Townsend
7. Peacock Lake
8. Lake Jeffery
9. Watertown Lake
10. Alligator Lake
11. Ocean Pond

Lake Carr is a very shallow body of water that approaches 400 acres when water levels are normal. It is loaded with lily pads and quite a few big bass. Fishing in the boat trails and openings in the bonnets will result in some after dark thrills here. You may want to use a shallow draft boat in this water hole for ease of navigation. A public ramp allows access.

MICCOSUKEE AND IAMONIA

Near Lake Jackson and Tallahassee is a 6,276 acre lake called Miccosukee. The sea of grass, located about 15 miles from the town of Monticello and the same distance from the state capital, is a good bass lake that is often overlooked by anglers. It still yields numerous trophy-size largemouth, despite posing the challenge of pulling such lunkers from extremely dense cover.

The 7-mile long lake was created in the 1950s by the construction of a dam on the north end. Several sinkholes exist in the area, and the lake was created to hold some water above ground. When the lake, averaging around eight feet deep, overflows

113

into the spillway, its water flows into one of the larger sinkholes in the area. Fishing the moving water in the spillway basin can pay off with some big bass. Otherwise, this is a boat angler's lake.

Since the lake is only one mile wide and very shallow, it is an exceptional night fishing lake. A lure cast in any direction will seemingly be in the "strike zone" all the way back to the boat. Most of the giants taken in the past few years were caught after dark. They come from the grass, pads, cattails and moss that live in abundance on these waters. You have about 15 miles of shoreline to cover, so there are plenty of potential bass spots.

Weedless lures are your only option on Miccosukee. Fish them at night or down the boat trails. On windy days, cast the flats and work spoons and plastic worms slowly through the thick cover. Check out the potholes isolated by grass in some areas. Water may be up to 7 feet deep in some. In the winter, try fishing shiners on weedless hooks for big bass action.

A paved launch ramp is available on highway 90 at Lloyd's Creek on the southern end of the lake. Lloyd's Creek is one that flows underground a short distance south of the ramp.

Just 12 miles north of Tallahassee off highway 319 and Lake Iamonia Road is the 5,757-acre Lake Iamonia. It has a dense covering of grass, lily pads and submerged vegetation. Fish the boat trails with topwater plugs early and late or toss weedless spoons in the vegetation pockets for best results.

OTHER OVERLOOKED BASS WATERS

The fishing on Ocean Pond is generally best at night or during overcast weather, when the wind picks up. The 1774-acre, clear-water lake located south of Olustee is round, shallow and with very little structure on its shores. Buoys identify fish attractors placed by the Game & Fresh Water Fish Commission and are good areas for bass concentrations. Weedbeds along the shores, grassy islands and huge cypress trees are good bass attractors as well.

A public ramp is on the southern end of Ocean Pond. If you want to try for some sunshine bass in addition to largemouth near Lake City, try Watertown Lake. The 46-acre lake offers fertile water with extensive shoreline cover. Other area bass lakes around Lake City and Live Oak include the 338-acre Alligator Lake, the 148-acre Peacock Lake, the 114-acre, clear water Lake Jeffery, the 63-acre Suwannee Lake and the 110-acre Lake Townsend.

The bass of Lake Miccosukee are often fooled by a weedless rubber plug. With the dense vegetation, patience and heavy line are a must.

In Franklin County, southwest of Tallahassee, is St. Vincent Wildlife Refuge, a 12,350-acre island offering primitive freshwater fishing areas. It's located about five miles from the coastal city of Apalachicola and is accessible only by boat. The bass ponds can be reached from the island's east shoreline. Anglers should carry a small canoe or lightweight boat for portaging between ponds. The waters here are only open certain months, so contact the St. Vincent Wildlife Refuge, P.O. Box 447, Apalachicola, FL 32320 for complete details and island map.

LAKE JACKSON DETAILS

The Florida Game and Fresh Water Fish Commission recently placed a slot limit to restrict harvest of largemouth bass on the popular Lake Jackson. The regulation requires fishermen who catch bass between 13 and 17 inches long to return them immediately to the water unharmed. The slot limit is designed to help increase the number of big bass in the lake by encouraging more angler harvest of smaller fish and allowing intermediate-size fish to grow.

For guide information, contact Paul Tyre at 3030 Lakeshore Dr., Tallahassee, FL 32312 or phone (904) 385-2082.

12

APALACHICOLA'S SLOUGH SANCTUARIES

THE CHALKY WATER had a visibility of about one inch at best, yet I was casting plastic worms along the perimeter grass in Montgomery Slough, just off the Apalachicola River. Both the bass and I were on a "feeling expedition," and they were finding the bait with regularity. After only two hours of fishing, I had caught seven largemouth.

The action on small largemouth was interesting, but the times got more exciting when a one-pound bluegill leaped from the surface, ahead of our boat. My partner surmises that the panfish was after a May fly or other terrestrial.

"I believe that small fish was being chased," I said as I cast a topwater plug toward the 'forage.' "I'll check it out."

Oysters aren't the only attraction. For largemouth bass action in a salty bay, you can't top these waters!

The 3-inch surface lure had just splashed down where the descending bluegill should have been when it was engulfed in a huge boil. The immediate strike from the predator proved the value of my decision to cast at the commotion.

After a short battle, I lipped the 7 pound, 10 ounce largemouth. It was a fine photo fish, with a backdrop of numerous bayous, sloughs, and small hidden waterways just off the Apalachicola River. I've been back since to the cream coffee-stained waters and have done well.

The Apalachicola River system offers several streams that are just wide enough for a boat, and those generally have the fresh water bass habitat that many anglers pass up. For those bass anglers with a desire to explore the small hidden areas off the main river channel, a nice surprise awaits. There are plenty of small tributaries available for exploration, and to the north, the river is wide.

The big river below Lake Seminole has a relatively brushy bottom, and its outer bends are points of wood pileups. Trees line the river, and the constant current slowly erodes the bank and eventually washes root-bound dirt away. The shoreside timber then topples into the deep water and is washed to the bottom.

The most frequent cause of the brushy river bottom is wind. Hurricanes and tornadoes are both frequent visitors to this part of the state. Such storms can knock down multitudes of water-lined trees. As the banks cave in, the Apalachicola River channel is widened with the deeper water still on the outer bend. The submerged brush lying in the bend attracts game and food fish.

As you cruise the river, it is not difficult to spot the points along shore where a possibility of submerged branches or timber exists. Wind-downed trees on many banks are very easy to find. On the very deep bends, a densely-branched, submerged tree may offer several fish to an angler from the very same spot.

The river banks with numerous logs and stumps provide eddy areas, and they in turn provide good ambush points for bass to grab a careless baitfish. An eddy can be productive with current swept baits on either an outgoing or incoming tide, but the river may change from one tide to the other.

Deep outer bends along the Apalachicola are consistent on either tide, but the nature of the run just above and below it often determines the current speed on each tidal phase. A sharp bend immediately in front of the bend would slow the current action, while a long straight run could speed it up.

EXPLORATIONS AND DISCOVERIES

I recently had an opportunity to fish the area with Shag Shahid, a tackle manufacturer's representative who has some 28 years experience on the waters. Shahid believes in going where others can't, so he has really explored the tributaries off the Bay. His boat has been pushed, pulled and winched over huge logs that tides expose at least once a day. His outboard will kick up as the rig slides over such obstructions.

In some of the sloughs, he has stuck his boat on blown-over tree trunks for several hours.

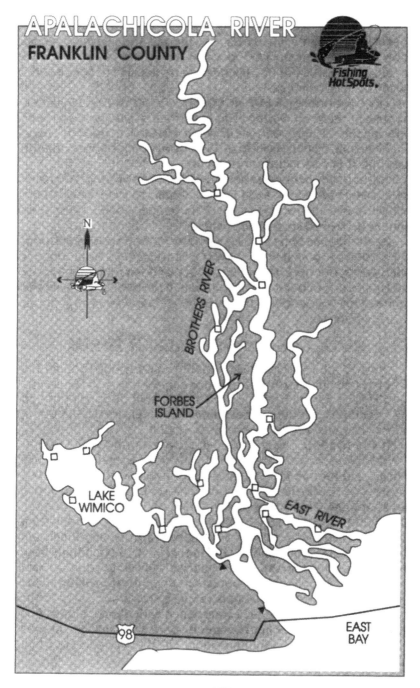

APALACHICOLA RIVER

FRANKLIN COUNTY

Fishing
Hot Spots.

N

BROTHERS RIVER

FORBES
ISLAND

LAKE
WIMICO

EAST RIVER

98

EAST
BAY

119

"It sometimes takes that long to get my boat off a tree stump," he said as we slowly vaulted over a couple and plopped down on the other side. "We mostly have to watch the tides though. When we go into a place like this on high tide and try to come out on the low, we could be in trouble."

The tidal influence and his preferred areas to fish depend on the time of the year. Spring brings southern winds and sometimes only one tide. The wind from the south will blow in the water from Apalachicola Bay all day long. When the brackish water finally goes out, it is very fast and turbulent.

"Most fishermen don't know how to handle swift water," claims the Alabama resident, "but I love it. When the water is swift, the fish will move and be able to get more oxygen. When the oxygen content increases, so does the fishing."

It follows then that two tides would be an even better condition, and according to Shahid, it is. Water movement in twice and out twice keeps the oxygen content higher and bass anglers usually catch fish on both tides. It is wise to watch the tidal action near the mouth of the Apalachicola to determine what will soon be going on in the tributaries.

CUTS, CREEKS AND FALLEN TREES

Most of the cuts and creeks twisting and turning through the river bay flats have visible obstructions at low tide that can usually be skirted or passed over when the tide is high. Passage through the tributaries, though, is not to be taken lightly. Use caution, unless you know the water as well as Shahid.

If you fish every week like he does, you'd probably be able to cite the history of each tree partially blocking a small slough. He told me that the one we got lodged on for five minutes was knocked down six weeks earlier by a hurricane. I was more concerned with catching some largemouth in my limited time, though.

We did catch two nice bass just a few hundred feet away from the overturned log. A smaller boat moved through the slough and passed us, which ended our fishing in that spot. Shahid pulled the trolling motor from the water and we moved to another less crowded channel. With many of the waterways off the Apalachicola just a few boat widths, two boats can be a crowd.

Our next spot where a cut intersected with a small slough was quickly cherished. Within five minutes, we each had caught four largemouth, including a four pounder. The tide was going out, and the bass were feeding on our plastic worms.

Bass from the Apalachicola estuaries are fat and healthy due to their protein-rich diet. Crankbaits account for many of the largemouth.

Shahid seemed to know right where they would be. He "follows the fish" on almost a daily basis. He can usually stay right on top of them and catch them every time out. Fortunately, in this area there is normally very little pressure on the fish during the week.

Limited boat traffic in the Apalachicola's brackish tributaries, away from the panhandle region's major population centers, is not unusual. The majority of the fresh water bass anglers in the sand hills of north Florida are attracted to the numerous inland lakes and ponds. Seldom are the "sweet-water" anglers even knowledgeable about the tidal effects on coastal bass.

121

WEATHER, FORAGE & TIDAL INFLUENCES

The productivity of these brackish waters is more consistent and often surpasses that of inland waters. Apalachicola estuaries are teeming with bass forage such as fingerlings of both salt and fresh water fish, shrimp, crabs, snails and salamanders. Around October, the creeks are full of migrating shrimp and the largemouth follow the forage.

Feeding bass are often as numerous as the forage, but an understanding of tidal influences may be necessary to take advantage of the opportunity. Barometric pressure, established primarily by the moon's orbit, affects tides on the earth's surface. Bodies of water are moved about, causing changes in water level, temperature and clarity.

Tides dry up shoreline habitat during low periods and then sweep estuary forage along in their current. The effects of drought over the bay region vary, depending on the flowage rates of tributaries. In the dry season, saltwater intrusion from the nearby bay can pose a problem to bass in the sloughs and cuts near the Gulf. The shorter ones with limited flow can be rendered essentially useless for freshwater bass angling then.

Such weather conditions are especially critical in the Apalachicola's estuary waters since tidal phases and water level changes are minimal. Heavy rains, on the other hand, can lower the pH and salinity of brackish water and move tidal bass closer to the sea. Winds, too, can accelerate or reverse tidal current flow, making the feeding activity unpredictable.

Falling tides offer, in general, the most productive tidal bass fishing. The water movement also makes the water dingy and helps the bass fishing. It's usually clear, though, around the mouth of the watershed, unless a bad storm has come through.

Baitfish are forced out of their hideouts by falling tides into deeper waters. Weaker swimmers are less mobile than their predators in the fast currents and are easy targets then. Bass normally feed voraciously on the falling tide until the current speed approaches zero.

After a lull during slack tide, the Apalachicola bass proceed to feed on the incoming tidal currents with somewhat less vigor until the marshy flats are flooded. At high tide, top water plugs can be productive and small spinners will occasionally entice feeders from the grass. Feeding activity again slows near the high slack tide and generally remains dead until the tide is falling rapidly.

TACTICS, LURES & BAIT

Plastic worms, particularly those that are scent-impregnated, like Berkley's Power Worms, fool their share of the strong fighting bass in the marshy river bends until the tide has fallen so much that mud banks and shoreline weeds lay exposed. Then, floating balsa lures retrieved across the shallow flats can account for largemouth. Bass can then often be found on the quick drops, just off the flats which give them a choice of depth and cover.

As the tide continues to fall, successful anglers switch back to plastic worms. They probe the deep outer bends of the cuts and creeks off the main river channels. The bass are generally there. They hold on whatever structure is available.

Cuts where the marsh areas feed into the tidal creeks and sloughs are prime spots in the area to catch a mess of fish. These runins congregate baitfish and bass will be there during an outgoing tide, even if it only occurs one time each day. Shahid prefers big, deep-running crankbaits for such areas, particularly in the cooler months. He's caught several bass weighing over seven pounds on the plugs.

SALTWATER INTERACTIONS

It won't matter what type lure you are tossing if some "sportsmen" happen to be in front of you on one of the small waterways. Three tidewater haul netters happened in front of local resident Richard Bolin and I several years ago while we were black bass fishing one of the sloughs in the area.

We had only been on the water about two hours and were working a fresh water cut from the river toward the salty East Bay when we heard two outboard motors start up just ahead of us. Soon, the two boats rounded the bend in our direction until one of them moved ahead and across the small creek, stretching a net taut between them. The water lying ahead of us was muddied for at least a mile, and our fishing for the morning was, in effect, shot.

The weekend "fishermen" were haul netting for salt water fish, but I wonder how many largemouth are killed by their technique. Their salt water "sport" was legal up to a railroad bridge on the Apalachicola River, and the area unfortunately also encompasses several miles of superb fresh water fishing. The Apalachicola is relatively unspoiled and unpolluted, but instances as above endanger this condition.

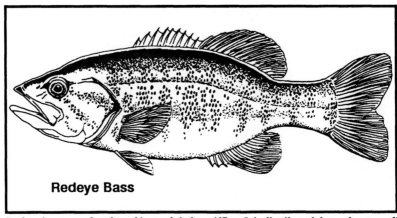

Redeye Bass

Redeye bass are often found in pools below riffles. It is distributed throughout small rivers in North Florida.

RIVER BASS SPECIES

The relatively unknown bass species in the river system are the sporty spotted *(Micropterus Punctulatus)*, redeye *(Micropterus Coosae)*, and shoal *(Micropterus Family)* bass. Their range is very restricted, but they do well in their own endemic environment in this system. The three minor bass species are neglected, but that is due more to lack of fishing knowledge by the anglers. The fish certainly fight pound for pound, once hooked.

Redeye, called "coosa bass" in some circles, and spotted bass, are more closely related to the smallmouth bass than to the largemouth. Many of the habitats, forage preferences, and successful catching techniques for the minor bass species are similar. Also, redeye bass, like the other two species, seldom grow to more than one pound. In fact, a one-year old redeye bass may average only two inches in length and a ten-inch specimen would probably be eight years old, according to fisheries biologists.

The redeye bass are usually found in clear-flowing, upland streams off the Apalachicola River and its main tributary, the Chipola. It has been called the "brook trout of the warmwater game fish" since it is comparable in size and inhabits fast-moving waters which are too warm for trout.

The redeye is a colorful bass with a deep bronze back, mottled with olive green bands. The eyes are generally dark red to a brownish red and the dorsal, anal, and caudal (tail) fins are reddish also. Opaque white and bronze markings on the tail fin are usually

124

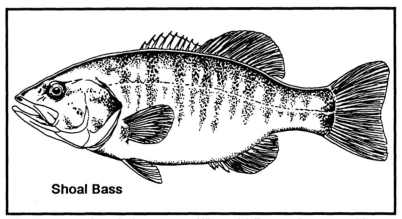

Shoal bass usually prefer large stream riffles and fallen wood structure. They are strong fighters for their size

distinct. The underside of the bass often takes on a deep, bluish hue, as do streaks down the sides of the upper jaw. The fins and location of the catch are generally the basis of identification of a redeye bass.

Feeding heavily on terrestrial insects over most of their lifespan, the redeye switches more to a crustacean diet as it grows to larger sizes. They can be caught on a variety of small lures and live bait. Small spinners are top redeye attractors, as are small crankbaits in white, crayfish, chrome or chartreuse colors.

An ultralight spinning outfit is ideal for anglers pursuing this fish. The short rod is well suited for the shrub-lined stream banks and six-pound test monofilament should suffice for battling the redeye. Fly rodders should limit the length of their rod to seven feet and use a number five or six double taper or weight-forward floating fly line. Cast upstream and let the current help your lure or bait back across the pool.

Redeyes prefer a river stream section that offers a steep grade (10 to 20 foot drop per mile) with many riffles and pools. The quiet float fisherman or wader can usually catch a few in the remote stretches of short pools with fast current. Areas between runs and riffles are best.

CHIPOLA SPOTS AND SHOALS

The redeye's closest relative is the shoal bass. Some biologists believe that they both are distinct species, while others contend

The Apalachicola River headwaters also offer large redeye bass for those anglers lucky enough to tangle with one.

the shoal bass is a subspecie of the redeye. The fish, also called Chipola bass, has never been given a scientific name, though. Its range in Florida is restricted to the Apalachicola River system, specifically to numerous fast-water limestone shoals in the Chipola River. The native redeye are most abundant in the upper portion of the river.

The scenic Chipola River originates in Houston County, Alabama near the Florida/Alabama state line, and winds some 97 miles south through slow rolling hills to its confluence with Florida's Apalachicola River. Along its length, it has helped form intricate cave systems, including the Florida Caverns State Park in Marianna, one of the largest in the United States. Because it's spring fed and has a limestone bottom, the Chipola River is one of the clearest in the state. Its name means "sweet water" in Indian dialect.

The river averages five to 15 feet deep and is very scenic with cold, fast-water shoals. Huge oaks and cypress trees line the limestone banks and there are many rocks and fallen logs along the way. The northern portion, from Marianna to Highway 20, is navigable only on high water. Small bass boats can ply the 30 miles between Florida 20 south to Dead Lake, however, throughout the year. With a larger bass boat, watch out for the narrow, fast water channels.

Largemouth bass can be found around the grassy beds and in calmer waters. Use crankbaits, spinner baits and Snagless Sally type lures for best results. Weedless lures are often used around the heavy shore cover. Due to its clear waters, lighter line is more productive. In cold weather, between January and March, single blade spinnerbaits are preferred because they sink quicker. Bass will be found then in the deeper channels, so crankbaits fished in six to eight foot depths are also productive. In the spring, weedless plastic worms and spinners produce bass when fished around the grass beds. In the summer, topwaters work early and late in the day.

The shoal bass is found in rapids along the lower Apalachicola drainage, where it feeds predominantly on crayfish and small baitfish. The state record for the brightly-colored black bass is seven pounds. The bass can be differentiated from the redeye by a prominent spot right before the tail and another on the edge of the gill cover, and an absence of white on the upper and lower edges of the tail fins.

Preferring clear-water riffle areas, the shoal bass consequently has a discontinuous distribution throughout its range. The Chipola River's large stream habitat with food-intensive shoals are conducive to shoal bass growth. The fish rarely move out of the fast flowing stream habitat and prefer stream widths of 75 to 100 feet. Prime bottom characteristics are a mixture of sand, rubble and limestone outcropping.

SPOTTED SPOTS

Spotted bass prefer the larger stream and river habitats of the Apalachicola with medium current, temperate water, and visibility averaging three to six feet. Their distribution also includes the Escambia (upper River), Blackwater, Yellow, and Choctawhatchee Rivers in northwestern Florida. The northern spotted bass is the subspecies introduced into the Apalachicola drainage.

The Apalachicola River is probably the best spotted bass water in Florida. The fish only grows to six or seven years of age, and the state record, caught June 24, 1985 by Don Gilmore, of Chipley, is a 3-pound, 12-ounce specimen from the Gulf County portion of the Apalachicola. The spotted bass struck a Bagley Killer Bee II crankbait. It measured 18 1/4 inches in length and was 13 1/2 inches in girth.

The fish bear longitudinal rows of spots, with younger specimens showing the irregular dark lateral stripe of the largemouth ending at a spot at the base of the tail. Other distinguishing marks are a connected first and second dorsal fin, and an upper jaw bone that does not extend back beyond the eye. Check also for small black spots below the lateral line on the rear edges of scales and for small teeth on their tongues.

Crayfish are naturally a favorite morsel, but shad (when available) and small sunfish frequently are on the spot's menu. Plastic worms, grubs, jigs and small, deep-running crankbaits in dark earth tones are good choices for fooling a spotted bass along rocky stretches of a stream. Cast the artificials or the real thing (crayfish) to rocky structure.

RIVER AREA DETAILS

The Chattahoochee and Flint Rivers of southern Georgia become one below Lake Seminole and the Jim Woodruff Lock and Dam at the town of Chattahoochee, Florida and form the Apalachicola River. The Apalachicola flows south about 190 miles to the Gulf of Mexico. Water levels are maintained by the U.S. Army Corps of Engineers dam and seldom fluctuate more than two feet.

The river winds its way south to the delta just west of the National Forest by the same name. It is a fairly large and deep waterway, but its tributaries are generally small and oft shallow. The area can be reached on State Road 98 west of Tallahassee at the town of Apalachicola.

Near the mouth at the Gulf, the tidal ecosystem discharges brackish water into the Apalachicola Bay. There are about 50 fresh water streams and rivers in the vicinity flowing into the Apalachicola River. Tributaries in the middle portion of the Apalachicola include Old River, Outside Lakes, Equaloxic Creek, Larkin Slough, River Styx, Kennedy Creek and numerous other sloughs and streams. In the lower portion, Montgomery Slough, East River, Brothers River, Howard Creek, Brickyard Cutoff and Owl Creek are all good bass waters connected to the river.

On the lower river, several marinas offer launching for a small fee. One launch site is on Brothers River at Willis Landing. On the upper river, a free public landing is located off Highway 71 near Wewahitchka. For more information on accommodations and marinas, contact the Apalachicola Chamber of Commerce..

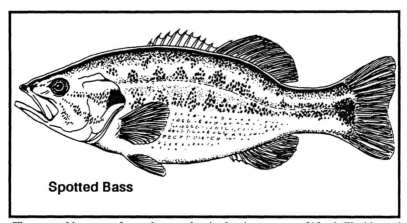

Spotted Bass

The spotted bass opts for rocky stretches in the river waters of North Florida and generally grows only to four pounds or so. It finds its preferred forage, the crayfish, readily available there.

The Apalachicola River in the panhandle is one of the top waters in the state for sunshines. A previous state record (15 pounds, 10 ounces) was caught there in April of 1985. For more details on the striper and hybrid striper fishery, refer to the Lake Seminole chapter on the two fish. Anglers who want to know more about the striper fishery can call the Apalachicola National Estuarine Research Reserve or the Florida Game and Fresh Water Fish Commission.

13

EXCITING
SPRINGS AND STREAMS

VAST DEPOSITS OF limestone exist on land areas that were once covered by the ocean. In this region of northern Florida and southern Georgia, both springs and sinkholes are numerous.

Many springs are sources of large, navigable rivers, with mouths often 100 feet across. Thousands of lesser springs and sinkholes are also found in most of the river systems. The "belt" is bounded on the north by Valdosta and Waycross, Georgia, and on the east by the St. Johns River. The range extends westward through the panhandle and south almost to Orlando. The territory includes several watersheds where the fishing can be exciting.

The "Limestone Spring Belt" offers beautiful scenery and great bass fishing in moving waters!

More than 20 Florida springs in the "belt" area discharge at least 65 million gallons of water daily. The springs erupt from ground water through the lime deposits. As limestone is washed away, cavities are formed through the soil, resulting in the development of runs and sinkholes.

Sinkholes are formed as the water is 'sucked' into the earth. When surface water trickles down through a thin crust of lime to a cavity below, the structure weakens and a cave-in results. The underground water action, formed when a head of pressure builds and pushes water to the surface, gives birth to 'runs.'

Float fishing one of the spring runs of Florida can be a beautiful and rewarding experience. Largemouth bass are numerous in these river systems. Spring-influenced river systems are often characterized by limestone banks, rocky shoals and strong currents. A canopy of moss-draped cypress, oak and maple is fairly common to the region's narrow, twisting river banks. Shoals and shallows often limit boat traffic near the headwaters of tributaries. The downstream ends are very navigable, however,

A pleasant float trip is usually possible on most watersheds in the limestone region. Spring upwellings through the limestone caverns in many of the waterways in north Florida and south Georgia initiate substantial currents that can quickly sweep a boat downstream. Fishing the heavy currents is a unique challenge. The limestone shoals will play havoc on the tackle, and the angler will often have to crank up the outboard and motor back upstream to retrieve a snagged lure.

Most spring runs are clearest during low water. Rates of flow in the runs will vary with the fluctuating water table, as does the water level. Even in the stained river systems, the water is generally clear in the fall and winter. Algae during the summer rainy season will normally darken the water. Springs near the banks of surface rivers will also become very dark during periods of heavy rainfall.

Most spring runs in the region contain largemouth bass of up to 12 pounds, and many other springs yield particularly impressive specimens as well. Bass weighing 15 pounds have been caught from the Apalachicola and Econfina Rivers in this limestone spring "bass belt." These rivers are well-known for their fishing opportunities, but they are just a few of the many waterways spawned from the spring/sinkhole network in Florida's limestone base.

MEANDERING WATERWAYS

The Chipola River, which feeds the Apalachicola, offers shallow and crystal clear waters flowing over a limestone bed. While it is enjoyable to drift and cast for the rare shoal (coosa) bass, the water clarity makes angling especially challenging.

Another well known tributary is the small, undeveloped Withlacoochee River which flows from Quitman, Georgia for about 30 miles to its junction with the Suwannee River near Live Oak, Florida. This spring-influenced river has good largemouth and Suwannee bass fishing. While it is navigable only by canoe, there are plenty of small bass to enjoy along the way. In the winter, the high waters even create one of Florida's few white water rapids at Melvin Shoals.

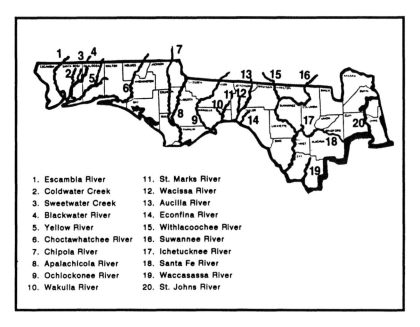

1. Escambia River	11. St. Marks River
2. Coldwater Creek	12. Wacissa River
3. Sweetwater Creek	13. Aucilla River
4. Blackwater River	14. Econfina River
5. Yellow River	15. Withlacoochee River
6. Choctawhatchee River	16. Suwannee River
7. Chipola River	17. Ichetucknee River
8. Apalachicola River	18. Santa Fe River
9. Ochlockonee River	19. Waccasassa River
10. Wakulla River	20. St. Johns River

Scuba diving and canoeing are other sports that are participated in extensively on the Ichetucknee River near Branford. The beautiful six miles of the Ichetucknee provides thousands of weekend tube-floaters an opportunity to spend several hours drifting by unspoiled wilderness. The lower three miles offers angling for the numerous, but very wary, largemouth and Suwannee bass.

West of Tallahassee, the Ochlockonee River, although not crystal clear, is fertile and the bass can grow large. The river runs through Lake Talquin on its way to the Gulf. Stripers are attracted to the spillway below the dam in the first few cold months of the year.

ST. MARKS AND WAKULLA

Other spring-influenced rivers with excellent bass angling exist in the 'belt.' In the panhandle region, the Wakulla, St. Marks and Aucilla Rivers are noteworthy fishing streams. These and other spring-influenced tributaries often provide excellent bass angling.

The spring-fed St. Marks and Wakulla rivers are located 15 miles south of Tallahassee. The Wakulla flows into the St. Marks and continues for about 7 miles toward the Gulf. The source of the

Wakulla is one of the world's largest springs - Wakulla Springs - now a state park. It is a fairly broad, shallow river which accommodates very small boats or canoes better than larger fishing boats. Boats can navigate as far as four miles below the spring before encountering the boundary of the state park.

The best bass times here are during the spring and summer, although the constant water temperature does provide good fishing year round. The heavy aquatic vegetation on the Wakulla is excellent bass cover. Plastic worms in chartreuse or black colors, rigged weedless or Carolina, and spinnerbaits with yellow and white skirts are productive.

The St. Marks River originates in a swamp east of Tallahassee and offers waters 10 to 15 feet deep in some areas. Its shorelines are mostly hardwood forests and swamps, providing excellent cover and forage base for bass. At the junction of the Wakulla and the St. Marks are two launch sites/marinas, but fishermen may want to boat upstream to locate the better bass angling.

TACTICS FOR RIVER FISH

All waters mentioned contain largemouth, several have spotted and/or redeye and a few provide rare Suwannee bass to anglers. The smaller bass species normally prefer limestone rapids and shoals, gushing springs, sinkhole areas and swift currents. They are most comfortable in the neutral pH levels (around 7.0 on the pH meter) and narrow water temperature ranges (usually 68 to 74 degrees) provided by the spring waters. Largemouth bass, however, prefer quieter sites such as the pad fields and fallen timber along the banks.

Spring bass love crayfish, which composes a majority of their diet. They will hit most of the lures that resemble such morsels and, like most river bass, will wallop artificials fished super slowly and near the bottom.

The best time of the year to fish the river systems is during high water periods, due to the presence of bottom-scraping shoals in most. Late spring through October is a good time to find adequate water and plenty of bass. The rivers' temperature will remain fairly cool in mid-summer, providing day-long angling activity even when the afternoon sun bears down.

The underground network of waterways in the limestone spring bass belt is complicated. The two dozen major spring-influenced rivers running across the surface are not. Fishing for bass in the high-visibility waters normally encountered in them can be relatively easy and successful.

WESTERN PANHANDLE RIVER OPTIONS

Superb fishing opportunities exist in a beautiful serene untouched forest near Pensacola. The Blackwater River State Forest, a sprawling 183,000-acre recreational refuge, is primitive river bass fishing at the finest. Far from crowds, this is the largest state forest and yet remains unspoiled for all anglers to enjoy. The forest includes a 30-acre State Park with some 30 miles of nature trails through lush forest lands and around three natural lakes full of bass. The park also offers bridle trails, camping and wildlife education courses. The main attraction, though, is the river itself.

The Blackwater River originates in Alabama and flows for about 58 miles, through the Blackwater River State Forest and the heart of Florida's western highlands, before emptying into Blackwater Bay on the Gulf of Mexico. The Blackwater River, Coldwater Creek and Sweetwater Creek are spring fed. The clear waters require very light tackle and good sneaking skills to avoid spooking bass while float fishing.

The Blackwater fishing experience wanders through unsurpassed natural beauty. Bass up to five pounds abound in the crystal waters surrounded by tree-studded banks and white, sandy beaches. Several stretches of the river are too shallow during the dry season. Part of Florida's Canoe Trail System, the river is particularly conducive to fishing from canoes and lightweight craft. The trail begins at highway 180, two miles south of the state line and ends at the state park near Milton.

Logging bridges that once spanned the Blackwater River, canopies of cedar trees, maple and towering cypress and high bluff areas add adventure to the exciting bass action that most anglers experience. The river offers largemouth and spotted bass, as do the panhandle tributaries; Escambia (upper River), Yellow, and Choctawhatchee Rivers.

ESCAMBIA'S DELTA BASS

The Escambia River flows 54 miles through the panhandle into Escambia Bay at Pensacola. The marsh at its mouth is usually brackish in summer and early fall, but seasonal rains cause its water to freshen during winter and spring months. Even though the salinity is relatively high, the marsh, with its network of grass-laden canals and creeks, supports a fishable population of largemouth throughout the year. In fact, research has shown that bass are more abundant in the marsh than in the upper river or backwater areas.

Anglers have found that success (bass per hour) is about that of the rest of the state, but the fish's average weight is generally lower. A 12-inch bass is about average, and tests have shown that it takes about three years for the fish to grow that large. Due to the saltwater influence, bass here have different growth rates, perhaps dependent on their dietary habits. They prey heavily on crabs.

In the upper Escambia, anglers willing to forego easy navigation are treated to scenic surroundings and often good bass fishing. In fact, the river's largest bass are probably in this section. Sometimes bass up to 5 or 6 pounds are taken. The best areas are the mouths of tiny tributaries that feed the river. Bass often wait for food at these junctions.

The Escambia begins as a tiny creek just north of the state line and winds south. There are dozens of creeks, sloughs and ponds on either side of the river, and there are few launching facilities in the upper portion. Popular access points exist at Quintette, Molino, Century, Highway 90 and McDavid, but many may require a small boat and/or 4-wheel drive vehicle.

Strong currents in the upper section make a powerful trolling motor necessary, and during the warmer months, most of the bass are in the main river channels. Most bass year around are caught in waters less than five feet deep and around the lily pads, reeds, eel grass and fallen brush, in the shallow waters.

Most of the water color is stained and with all the cover, heavy tackle is very suitable here. Spinnerbaits and plastic worms are top producers on the upper river. Just keep them wet. Hit the incoming ditches, creeks and cuts, and hang onto the rod.

The Yellow River in Okaloosa County can be best reached at U.S. highway 90 near Milligan and at Highway 2 near Oak Grove. This swift running river is 50 miles long, and all of it is ideally suited for float fishing for bass. The lower portions of the river are generally best for fishing in the spring. Bass fishing in the Yellow is most productive when using crankbaits and plastic worms.

CHOCTAWHATCHEE EXPOSURE

The Choctawhatchee, called "Choctaw" for short, is a little publicized river in Walton County. The winding river originates in

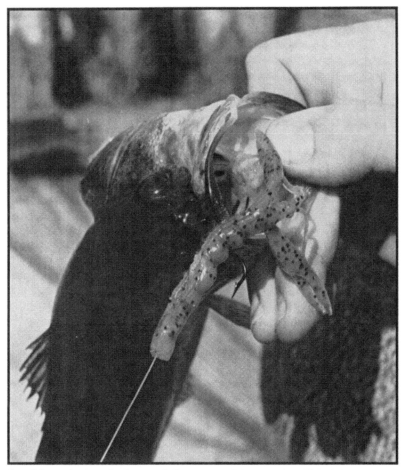

Crayfish are the favorite forage of all stream and river species of black bass. Small lures that closely resemble the morsels will attract the sporty fish.

Alabama and flows for approximately 80 miles through Florida's panhandle before reaching Choctawhatchee Bay. The lower portions of the river are more productive for bass, but lunkers are hard to come by. Three and four pounders are much more common than seven or nine pounders.

Largemouth are often pulled from the stickups and dead tree trunks along the river using crankbaits and plastic worms. During spring, the river floods, making it a challenge to find bass. With high water, the fish move back into the flooded swamps and are very difficult to find. Some of the best places to try at that time are the sloughs nearest the bay that are still emptying into the river.

There are about 150 miles of shoreline in the lower end, and the average depth is six or seven feet. The flooded marshland is also a good area to fish in the late spring, especially if the grass has not yet appeared. Find the creeks feeding into the river. These are not affected by the muddy waters of the river. For the best productivity, fish the river when it's low and the bass have to return to the main river channel from the swamps.

A plastic worm rigged weedless normally attracts a good share of largemouth. The key is to fish the worm fast, as these creek bass don't waste any time when they hit. If vegetation is present, such as milfoil, a spinner is also productive. Another effective lure to use between January and March is a single-bladed spinnerbait.

Black Creek, which drains into the Choctawhatchee River, sometimes attracts schools of striped bass as well as largemouth feeding on surface shad. At that time, a topwater lure can be exciting. The winter months are also good times to toss big-lipped crank baits, especially those in shad or crawfish colors. As early spring changes to late spring, the fish will move into shallower water. Then, shallow running artificials will be the ticket for largemouth.

In a novel project to create more habitat on the river, fisheries personnel have created a 20-tree fish attractor. It was placed about five miles north of the highway 20 bridge in a 400-yard stretch along the western shore just above Cedar Tree Landing. The oak and water hickory are anchored to the bank with half-inch steel cable to prevent them from floating down river in high water. This is the first time the Commission has placed a fish attractor in a river.

Several saltwater species come into the lower parts of the Choctawhatchee. In July, though, largemouth and spotted bass can be found in the brackish waters near the bay as they feed on migrating saltwater shrimp. There are several launching ramps along the remote river. Primary access is from a marina located in the delta area, which can be reached from Florida highways 20 or 79, and U.S. highways 98 and 231.

SHORT AND SWEET BASS FLOWS

The Waccasassa River is 29 miles long with a drainage area of 610 square miles. The name originates from a Seminole Indian phrase meaning "where there are cows" with "wacca" meaning 'cattle' and "sasi" meaning 'there are.' There are also largemouth bass in the remote waters. The Waccasassa runs through Levy County, which has the lowest population density in the state.

The river's high concentration of tannins and organic acids from swamps and forests give the water its dark color. About three quarters of the upper river portion is accessible only by canoes. The last seven miles downstream are accessible to small bass boats. There are a couple of boat ramps available - a county ramp three miles west of U.S. 19 and a private launch site.

In the Big Bend area, the Wacissa River is noted for its clear, cold water, wild beauty, and winding course through tall cypress stands. Only 15 miles long, it originates in a number of springs known as the Wacissa Springs Group, the largest being Big Blue Spring. The river can be accessed from highway 59 at the town of Wacissa. A public campsite is off U.S. highway 98 east of the Aucilla River bridge.

The best bass fishing is during the spring and summer months. A good method is to drop a plastic worm in the current and let it sink with the current. A heavy sinker may be necessary during higher water and faster moving current. Bass usually lie under snagged floating vegetation; as the worm sinks, the current will carry it underneath the vegetation to the waiting bass.

The most productive bass haunts include stands of cypress knees, along the edges of surface vegetation and the shores of small islands in the river - anywhere there's a sort of eddy away from the river current. Although the Wacissa is fairly wide, boat traffic is possible primarily through narrow channels in the vegetation. Boats on the Wacissa should be narrow, maneuverable and have a shallow draft.

PRIME LURES & BAIT

Discussing a 'typical' stream in this region may be misleading because seldom do they ever closely resemble each other. Successful bassin' techniques, however, tend to produce in all of them.

One favorite lure often used by locals is the Norman's Rip'N Minnow. Casts are timed to set the lure upstream of an overhanging structure, such as a limb or tree trunk. The lure is then allowed to drift into the bass-bearing cover. A twitch or two above the structure, and a submerged retrieve out of the cover once it reaches it, is effective.

Fallen and submerged trees and limbs are favorite spring bass haunts, and a plastic worm is a popular lure. Rising water can trigger bass into feeding binges where they will tear up every moccasin-colored worm in the tackle box, but timing is important. Once the water level has inundated the tree-lined banks, bass are difficult to locate, hot bait or not.

Altering retrieves and changing lure sizes as conditions warrant is important for angling success. Heavy rains and high water generally mean less clarity, larger lures and slightly heavier line required. A noisier retrieve might be more productive under these conditions.

Low water means highly spring-influenced conditions on many of these streams and clearer waters. The bass become more spooky and more difficult to trick into striking floating minnow imitators then. Boat and lure control may be more difficult as new structure rises above the spring run's surface. Worm-fishing at that time may be more productive.

As with any float trip, the entrance and exit locations should be planned in advance. Many anglers will embark at a downstream location, boat upstream to a selected spot and then drift back downstream a few miles to the convenient exit ramp. Most of the enjoyable fishing floats through the unspoiled spring runs take about an hour per mile.

Spring runs in the limestone region of Florida offer unique experiences and lots of bass to those in the know. Newcomers, however, should find a boat with a chipped or scratched hull and simply follow it!

140

14

NORTHEAST
POND ACTION

THE SOFT BOTTOM sucked at my tennis shoes as I tried to back out of the waist-deep waters. The seven pound bass was fighting on her terms, moving from one potential weed entanglement to another. Fortunately, during the battle I was able to lead it away from the weed clumps scattered along the point I was fishing.

I felt more comfortable in the knee-deep waters trying to land the fish, but the bass was still "green." She swam into possibly the last shallow grassbed near shore and stopped. I kept a tight line as I waded toward her. Then, suddenly, the fish became free of the obstruction and headed right toward me.

Catch these largemouth while wading, tubing, walking the bank or from a johnboat or raft!

The reel handle was seemingly a blur while I tried to reel in the slack. The bass with crankbait firmly affixed charged between my anchored legs. I was thinking of the treble hooks on the plug when the line cracked like a whip. The largest fish of the day was history, but I was out of a predicament caused by my attempt to "horse" a large, active bass.

I had caught nine bass while wading out to waist deep water on the small pond's gradually dropping point. Two fish were in the four pound class, and the others ranged from 14 to 17 inches. The day was a success without the seven pounder, but that's the fish that I would remember the most. The other battles and landings had gone by the book.

The resident largemouth in the three-acre pond near Keystone Heights were holding on the deeper weedbeds just off that point. There were no other points in the natural water, so the prime spot for me to cast was fairly obvious. I carefully approached the vegetation and cast my Big N past each clump of Johnson grass. As the billed lure wobbled by the grassbeds, a bass would occasionally pounce on it.

Such experiences are interesting and highly productive on the small, unnamed waters that pocket the upper two-thirds of the state by the thousands. Natural ponds are ideal to wade, since they seldom have surprises in the way of quick drops or unexpected submerged timber lying across the bottom. Soil is typically sand and relatively firm, and the primary structure in most is some form of vegetation.

Especially in the smaller ponds, largemouth react to variations in temperature, structure and pH levels. The angler that moves through the water wading, or with the aid of a float tube, can often discover the structure and thermal variance - without electronic equipment. A temperature difference of a couple of degrees can usually be detected even through rubber waders. A change in structure on one of these ponds may be pickerel weed to Johnson grass or bulrushes, and bass seem to concentrate at such spots.

When wade fishing or tubing a small pond, it's very important to analyze the water. The shoreline may be marshy in one area and deep in another. Cover could be abundant along one bank or point and sparse elsewhere. Fertility of the soil, denoted by the growth and height of vegetation in the natural bodies of water, is another parameter of importance to the productive angler; bass prefer nutrient-enriched areas with dense vegetation and forage possibilities.

Both wade fishing and tube fishing with the aid of a float tube involve a style not to be compromised by impatience. Moving slowly is actually an advantage on small waters, since the angler fishes each area more thoroughly than would the average boat angler. When the lure is presented repeatedly or closer to a bass, usually the chances are better for a strike.

SMALL POND FLOAT TACTICS

On another north Florida pond, I watched a "belly boater" position himself over one submerged rock pile and pull seven largemouth from it in less than 20 minutes. One weighed over

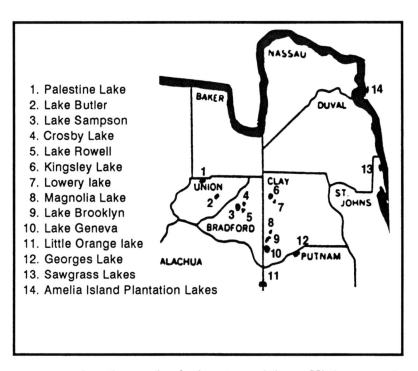

1. Palestine Lake
2. Lake Butler
3. Lake Sampson
4. Crosby Lake
5. Lake Rowell
6. Kingsley Lake
7. Lowery lake
8. Magnolia Lake
9. Lake Brooklyn
10. Lake Geneva
11. Little Orange lake
12. Georges Lake
13. Sawgrass Lakes
14. Amelia Island Plantation Lakes

seven pounds and a couple of others topped three. His home-made float tube was in about six feet of water. Many ponds have deeper waters that a tube fisherman can access. In fact, tubing is particularly suited for many north Florida barrow pits and other man-dug ponds.

The belly boat or float tube consists of an inner tube which is partially lined with a cloth material that protects the tube and provides a seat to straddle. The commercially-made covering and seat is usually made of nylon for rot and mildew resistance. While jeans and tennis shoes can be worn, chest-high waders will protect legs from underwater obstructions. Swim fins propel the craft in waters over waist deep.

The advantage of a wade fisherman or tube angler over a conventional boater is that he can access small waters most anywhere. Ponds typically without a launch ramp are great candidates for a "wet-fishing" expedition. Many Florida waters have perimeters of dense, impenetrable vegetation that neither the bank angler nor boater can access. Such waters lend themselves to the individual approach.

Soft-landing baits are usually most productive in tiny waters. The relatively-closed environment makes any "intrusion" easy to detect by those living within. Single-hook lures, like spinnerbaits, plastic worms, and grubs, provide a degree of safety when battling a feisty bass up close.

Most small, natural lakes in the state are shallow, and many are remote. The more remote, however, the more potential for coming face to face with a hazard. While you shouldn't worry needlessly about snakes and alligators, do respect them. Neither are usually aggressive, but it is just wise to keep your eyes open for water snakes and alligators and to avoid them.

Obviously, great care should be used when fishing water with possible dropoffs and deeper sections. To the wade fisherman, weather can be more of a problem than snakes or alligators. A lightning storm is something to respect, so get out of the water. Always heed the weather warnings.

Landing a fish when wading or tubing is normally easier than my experience mentioned above. In either case, you have to be very aware of your bait's hooks, but taking your time to play the fish is wise. Take along a small landing net for those potential lunker "problems," if you can call a big North Florida pond bass that.

TRAIL RIDGE LAKES

The lakes around Keystone Heights really get very little pressure but the bass fishing is often excellent. Anglers passing through the junction of highways 21 and 100 are usually on their way to one of the larger "name lakes" around Gainesville or Palatka. The so-called "Trail Ridge" lakes clustered around Keystone Heights, though, deserve recognition... when they are full of water.

Drought has plagued these lakes since the mid 1970's, and a rain shortfall over most years doesn't help the situation. Some of the little lakes that were 25 feet deep at one time have almost dried up over the years.

While droughts affect these waters rather substantially (I once had to back 100 yards further down the lakeshore to launch my bass boat at one lake), the fishing remains productive. The deep dimples in the sandy soil around Keystone Heights generally hold water and largemouth. Many of the 40 or so lakes and ponds have names and a few have ramps, but most are fished only by locals.

Finding a way to launch a boat on many of these waters can be difficult. Many are ringed by lots and lakefront homes, making

Residential, resort and golf developments provide a treasure of small waters in North Florida that are often overlooked by bass fishermen.

public access without an owner's permission impossible. On those lakes with access, the ramps are often poor, and a 4-wheel drive vehicle is advised if you are launching a full-size bass boat. A small aluminum boat or fiberglass two-man craft will fit the bill on most of these waters, however. Use a small outboard or powerful electric for mobility, a sonar unit and some deep-running baits, and you are properly equipped.

While living in Jacksonville several years ago, I visited the area often and found the typically small bass very eager biters. More than once, I was able to top my day's limit with a 6 or 7 pound largemouth. Lake records on some of the clear water bodies are over 15 pounds. Almost all of these lakes are spring-fed and connected to the Florida Aquifer.

Since the waters are gin-clear, the bass tend to hang offshore the short grass covering the bottoms in some waters. "Bank-runners" will not find a lot of success in most of the lakes, except during low-light times in the spring and fall. Those that drift or troll the open waters will usually be very productive, however. If you can fish offshore structure with light tackle, you may be in for the fastest action of your life. Twenty bass per person on some days is very possible. Summers are most productive on these deep little lakes.

AREA BASS LAKES

Lake Geneva, located on the east side of Keystone Heights, has a good ramp that is usable when the water level is normal. When the water is low, a private campground with hard sand beach allows easier access. This crystal-clear, 1,630-acre lake is one of the most productive in the area. Fish the grassy dropoffs in 8 to 10 feet of water for best bass action.

An excellent ramp exists off highway 100 on Lake Brooklyn, north of Keystone Heights, when the water level is normal. This lake is often the hardest hit by drought. Brooklyn is one of many lakes that drain into Etonia Creek which, in turn, dumps into Rice Creek on its way to Palatka and the St. Johns River. Sinkholes, however, drain off some of the water. The largest, according to hydrologists, is a 315-foot wide one at the bottom of the lake.

The deepest part of this 645-acre lake is about 35 feet, but most of the productive bass fishing takes place in waters around 10 feet. Deep-running crankbaits and Carolina-rigged worms are the best bet for largemouth action here.

The 1,263-acre Lowery Lake in the Camp Blanding Wildlife Management Area has a good ramp on its west side. Fishing in the super clear waters is best done at night. The lake is ringed by shoreline vegetation and has numerous brush piles along the maidencane grass beds. The bass average just over a pound in this lake, but there are a few monsters. Fish the edges of the grass and the brush after dark for best action.

Tiny Magnolia Lake is just 205 acres, but it does have a good ramp at the State Park off highway 21. This popular picnicking and swimming water is another good night-fishing lake. Like Lowery, the most productive areas here are along the maidencane grass in 6 to 8 feet of water.

The ponds on Sawgrass Resort are managed for fishing for the benefit of guests and development property owners.

Lakes Sampson and Rowell, located in Bradford County, are two good bass lakes that are connected by a small channel. Tiny Lake Rowell is surrounded by cypress trees which produce numerous bass in the spring. So do the fish attractors and underwater structure which are marked with buoys. They have been placed in the deep area of both lakes by the Game and Fresh Water Fish Commission.

The 2,042-acre Lake Sampson has several dropoffs which can be found with a depth finder. This underwater structure provides excellent bass habitat and schools of bass concentrate there during summer and fall. The best lures are Carolina-rigged plastic worms and deep diving crankbaits fished over the dropoffs. The dropoffs also attract their share of sunshine bass, and crankbaits are fair game for them also.

The hydrilla beds on Sampson are also productive. Fish the edges of the beds with plastic tube baits or use topwater plugs near the vegetation. When tossing plastic worms, spinnerbaits or spoons, let them sink into the holes and pockets in the vegetation.

Kingsley Lake, east of Starke, is a 1,652-acre water sports lake that is full of largemouth. Drifting a Texas-rigged worm in the middle away from the skiers and swimmers will bring fishing like you haven't seen for awhile. I spent several days on this water using the unique approach of fishing open water, dragging a worm along the bottom, and I caught numerous bass. They won't be large usually, but the action is consistent.

A couple of my favorite lakes in the area are Georges Lake and Little Orange Lake. On the former, I've released bass over 11 pounds back into the pretty, remote lake. It has a good depth off its sawgrass perimeter and also offers the estetics of cypress trees and other vegetation. A friend fishing with me on Little Orange caught and released a beauty over 10 pounds from the east shore one spring day. This lake is another sleeper with excellent bass fishing.

Palestine Lake (911 acres) and Lake Butler (420 acres) are two Union County waters that offer good bass fishing for smaller fish. Both are near the town of Lake Butler. The 558-acre Crosby Lake, located in Bradford County just west of Starke, offers yearling bass fishing also.

COUNTRY CLUB WATERS

Certainly most golfers have heard of the championship PGA golf course at Sawgrass, just south of Ponte Vedra Beach and north of St. Augustine. This area offers much more to the sportsman, in the form of great bass fishing ponds. Summer bass limits are easily obtained in the lagoon and water hazards that wind throughout the golf course. The country club lakes are maintained for fishing, but seldom does an angler place his boat on these waters.

The bulrush perimeter around most of the lagoons and waterways offer superb bass hangouts. Largemouth averaging 1 1/2 pounds are numerous at the edge of the drops, between the aquatic vegetation shelves and the deeper manmade lagoon waters. Scented Power Worms are preferred choices to interest the area bass. Rig them self-weedless with a slip sinker. Make a cast, and hang on to your rod, they're that thick.

A lake record of over 12 pounds makes these waters appropriate for the lunker hunters as well as for those looking for action. This place is great to peak the interest of a newcomer to fishing, and is highly recommended for that reason. Rental boats are available through the Golf Clubhouse and Activities Center. If you would

The author and Terry LaCoss are about to release these big bass back into the Amelia Island Plantation lake where they were caught.

like to bring your own craft, keep in mind that only resort guests or residents are allowed on these waters. A small johnboat and trolling motor is sufficient for exploring the golf links; no gasoline motors are allowed.

ISLAND BASS MAGIC

Amelia Island Plantation, about as far northeast in the state as a car will take you, is surrounded by beautiful oak hammocks and waterways that harbor heavyweight bass. Seldom do anglers have the opportunity to fish for such readily hungry largemouth. A beautiful professional golf course, numerous residential units and the scenic surroundings contain these mini bass waters.

On my initial trip to this area I fished with the Director of Fishing at the Plantation, Terry LaCoss. In a couple of hours, I caught nearly 30 pounds of bass, which were returned to the water for someone else to enjoy. Two fish over five, plus a seven pounder, highlighted an enjoyable day for this angler.

149

The fish at Amelia Island are extremely healthy, and forage is readily available to them. Bill Norman's Deep Big "N's" worked wonders for me on the man dug waters. The productive crankbaits should entice bass for most anglers working the brush laden shoreline. LaCoss favors worms, though, almost year round and has been quite successful with them. Boats entering these waters should have an electric motor for power.

Rental boats are not available at Amelia Island Plantation, but this experience can be enjoyed by only resort guests or by resident owner's friends. Again, a guide is not necessary on these waters as the visiting angler should do well without one.

FLORIDA POND ACTION

As days get shorter and the air temperatures reach refreshing marks, action can reach a peak in the small ponds that dimple north Florida. These small waters are the first to respond to weather alterations and the enterprising anglers should consider some of the hundreds scattered throughout this region of the state. Bass seem to become more active with cooler water.

There is probably a small body of water within ten miles of every angler in this region, yet most go overlooked. The cooler months are prime times to stop and fish that ditch you've been eyeballing all summer long or that neighborhood pond that seemed to attract every kid during summer vacation. You'll have most of the waters to yourself and you should catch some active fish.

Small plastic worms, crankbaits and spinners are deadly on the Florida largemouth that often average only a pound or two from such "micro-environments." More than once a lucky angler has been surprised by his "maxi" catch. Some of the largest bass inhabit tiny ponds in north Florida. They rule their environment and remain "unmolested" over most of their life. They can, indeed, provide a thrill for the small pond angler.

15

PANHANDLE'S
MINI-WATER BASS

MIST WAS BLOWING across the clear black water into the crude dirt ramp. A chill was in the air as Johnny Pate and I were preparing to launch his small aluminum boat.

The cool, humid air was quite unexpected then. I had left Lakeland the day before under clear skies and 85 degree temperatures. My two thin wind breakers were barely keeping me warm. The anticipated big bass action would, of course, help.

Sand pine and black oak scrubs ringed the 500 acres of seemingly 'transparent' waters. The cover was typical of most of the panhandle's spring-fed waters with low pH levels. It consisted of grass, pads and a hydrilla-type weed which provided adequate cover for the tiny freshwater shrimp that are vital to productive panhandle fisheries. The shrimp are the main ingredient in a bass' early life menu, and in small, clear waters, to an older bass.

Small waters with local reputations have plenty of giant largemouth action!

The biggest bass of the three-hour exploration struck within the first five minutes. A fish had boiled at my buzz bait as it encroached upon a pad bed. It cleanly missed.

A retrieve over the same territory angered a healthy four-pound largemouth that sucked in a Norman Triple Wing buzzer. The fish initially tried to "climb out of" the small lake and then headed for the wiry strands of aquatic weed on the bottom.

Several jumps later, I flipped the spunky bass aboard. That fish went into the live well for photos and release later, and we continued our search for big largemouth. We knew that they were there somewhere.

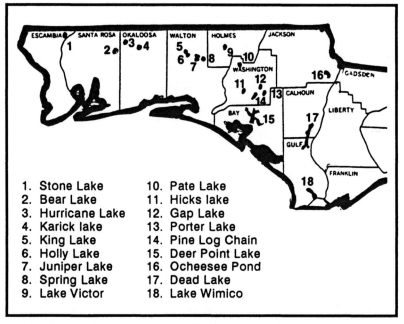

1. Stone Lake
2. Bear Lake
3. Hurricane Lake
4. Karick lake
5. King Lake
6. Holly Lake
7. Juniper Lake
8. Spring Lake
9. Lake Victor
10. Pate Lake
11. Hicks lake
12. Gap Lake
13. Porter Lake
14. Pine Log Chain
15. Deer Point Lake
16. Ocheesee Pond
17. Dead Lake
18. Lake Wimico

The little lake resembled many lunker waters in the six-county area. An average depth of 30 feet with a maximum of 50 are extremely common there. The annual water levels fluctuate drastically during the wet and dry times and the oft times clear waters dictate an even better night fishing spot.

We wouldn't have time on that trip to sample the after dark action. The nocturnal creatures of the backwoods would have to wait for another time to see us search those waters for a trophy largemouth under the moon. We made the best of it that morning, but time was too short.

We captured several more bass in the following three hours but none were bragging size. Our enjoyment, though, was in being miles away from a blacktop road and in releasing a couple of dozen chunky largemouth in short order. Plastic worms and the buzz baits produced well.

That small sand hill ponds and other many lakes and reservoirs that dimple the sandy soil in the panhandle are indeed the state's neglected largemouth 'holes.' There are hundreds of small ponds in Holmes, Washington, Bay, Calhoun, Walton and Jackson counties, a strip extending from the Apalachicola River westward past DeFuniak Springs.

Many panhandle anglers prefer the peace and solitude of bass angling on tiny sand hill ponds. The spunky dark-water bass often succumb to a tantalizing plastic worm or spinnerbait.

While many are private, some 25 percent of the little waters are open to the public, according to Freeport resident Johnny Pate. On others, an oral contract from visiting anglers is required to protect the water's anonymity.

That was true on this recent trip after panhandle bass. The gate keeper made it clear to us that we were not to mention in any form where we were about to fish that morning. Our experience there was no better than on others in public waters, but the fact remains that most of the public and private waters in the panhandle remain pretty much under-fished.

NIGHT OF BEHEMOTH BASS

In the spring of 1985, one of the largest bass ever caught in the state was taken from a small state-owned, yet "unnamed" panhandle pond. Donald Brunson of Geneva, Florida, caught the monster, and his fish might have had a legitimate shot at the 20-pound, 2-ounce state record had it not been out of the water for several hours before being officially weighed. It was caught around midnight and initially weighed on a produce scale at 19-pounds 2-ounces. Then, it was weighed again five hours later on certified scales at 18-pounds 8-ounces.

The 58-year old Brunson, a confirmed lunker hunter with several other big panhandle largemouth to his credit, including a 16-pounder, is after the next world record. He believes it will come from waters 30 miles either side of a line drawn from Juniper Lake to Lake Jackson, in the panhandle. Lakes Victor, Smith, Hurricane and several small mill ponds have all produced monster bass in years past. The typical mill ponds in south Georgia and northwest Florida have plenty of six-foot water and giant bass.

"I'll normally fish the shallow bedding areas where I can cast to the deeper stretches," Brunson says. "My favorite big bass bait is a black, 7-inch plastic salamander with a modified head. I like to fish it after dark. That's when I've caught most of my really big bass."

Florida undoubtedly produces more bass over 10 pounds than any other state. Usually, numerous 13 to 15-pounders are caught each year, but larger bass are rare. When giants near 18 pounds are caught, though, often it is from a small mill pond in north Florida. In a state with thousands of ponds, predicting which one will produce a monster is difficult.

SAND HILL PUBLIC WATERS

Those wishing to discover some of Florida's great reservoir fishing for heavyweight largemouth can find that in the panhandle too. Juniper, Holly, Dead Lake and others have built a local reputation for trophy fish, but the word is slow to spread. In a day and age when fishing pressure is often overwhelming and secrets difficult to keep, such an area is a rare find.

Fish management areas in the panhandle are numerous, and they are often hotspots for bass. Several lunker bass waters managed by the Game and Fresh Water Fish Commission exist in northwest Florida. Management waters that are often overlooked by big bass chasers include 58-acre Karick Lake, a 20-foot deep body of water in Okaloosa County; Stone Lake and Juniper Lake. They also include Hurricane Lake, where bass over 16 pounds have been taken in recent years.

Hurricane Lake yielded a 17-pound, 9-ounce largemouth to Robert Dunsford, of Jay, in the spring of 1984. The man was

Donald Brunson shows off his 18 1/2 pound largemouth that came from one of the panhandle's big bass ponds.

fishing alone in a small boat powered by an electric trolling motor when he saw the huge female on a bed in shallow water. He cast a jig and shad tail to the bed and the big bass fielded it. His 20-pound test line held as the lake record fish was finally subdued.

Dunsford's fish was just one of many large bass to come from the 350-acre lake. The small waters near the Alabama line in the Blackwater River State Forest also produced a 15 3/4 pounder to a biologist with the Game and Fresh Water Fish Commission and a 17 pounder to a Crestview angler the previous spring.

Hurricane Lake, located in the Forest, was opened to fishing in 1973, and during the winters of 1980 and 1983 was lowered five feet for revegetation purposes. The lake, formed when two small creeks were dammed, has waters 24 feet deep, but it is relatively sterile.

The lake has rich vegetation growth on the bottom today due to good water clarity and occasional doses of fertilizer. The lake has underwater springs, creek channels, standing timber, and even an old road bed. The bass fishing in Hurricane varies from good to poor.

155

Stone Lake in Escambia County was opened to fishing in 1969, and after a drawdown in 1979, has been producing good bass fishing. This 130-acre impoundment west of highway 29 was constructed solely for public fishing. A fishery management program consisting of lime application and liquid fertilization was initiated in the early 1980's, and that was followed by the stocking of threadfin shad a few years later.

Karick Lake was opened to fishing in 1966, and after a summer drawdown in 1977 to control aquatic plants, bass production increased substantially. Through the aid of a fertilization program in 1980, the number of bass per acre jumped. Dam repairs completed in the spring of 1986 required the total draining of the lake. Reflooding and restocking then has helped the lake come back to yield good bass fishing.

MORE OVERLOOKED WATERS

Lake Victor, a 130-acre lake in Holmes County, was opened to fishing in 1968. It was dewatered in 1970 and afterward produced a limited number of trophy-size largemouth. A nine-foot drawdown in 1986 exposed approximately 50 percent of the lake bottom. A fertilization program implemented after that has produced better bass fishing opportunities here. It is often overlooked.

Many more anglers from Alabama and Georgia fish panhandle waters with a non resident license than do Floridians from east of Tallahassee. It's closer. Jackson County borders the two states while Walton and Holmes counties abut Alabama. Many out of state anglers know that their best bet for a trophy fish lies 30 to 60 minutes away in Florida panhandle waters. Few Florida fishermen realize, though, what can be found a short drive to the west.

"Several of the numerous sand hill ponds have been taken from the public access holes," says Pate. "Timber companies own much of the land in the panhandle that used to be open to the public."

The generous permission extended to visiting anglers for many years had to be re-evaluated due to the influx of newcomers into the region, according to the Walton County native. The timber companies now lease some of the land to individuals or groups.

The larger 'ponds,' actually natural lakes of 200 to 400 acres, include Porter, Dunford, Crystal, Lucas, Gap, Hicks, Hammock, Hamilton, Wages, Pate, Rattlesnake Pond and the Pine Log Chain. Most are clear while some have a dark, transparent look. All offer excellent angling opportunities during normal water level conditions.

BIG AND LITTLE OPTIONS

Ocheesee Pond in Jackson County is 2,225 acres of gin clear water over a beautiful cypress swamp. Bass up to 15 pounds have been taken from these overlooked waters near the town of Sneads. Smith Lake, a 160-acre cypress bay lake in Washington County, has dark tannic-stained water and good spring bass fishing. The lower end of the lake was restored in 1977 providing some bank access.

Tiny Bear Lake in Santa Rosa County is just 107 acres, but since being opened to fishing in 1961, has produced a lot of 10 pound plus largemouth. It went through renovation and restocking in 1970, and a second drawdown in 1980 exposed approximately 50 percent of the lake bottom. A fertilization program initiated in 1987 has kept the pounds of bass per acre in Bear Lake to be above the norm for panhandle waters. Despite its size, waters near the dam are 24 feet deep, more than enough for bass to escape heat and cold extremes.

There are about 100 sand hill ponds in Washington County alone, and most are difficult to locate, so local directions are needed. Several of the named ponds lie off highway 77 between Chipley and Panama City. Access to most is by ungraded and unmarked sand roads, so a guide or a detailed map is advised for those type waters.

While some sand hill ponds have a nice, paved ramp, most have crude dirt launch areas. Launching a bass boat on many of the area's small ponds requires a 4-wheel drive vehicle. There are several other panhandle waters, however, that offer good largemouth bass fishing and have somewhat better launching facilities. Spring Lake, just 3 1/2 miles east of DeFuniak Springs, is just one such area.

A bass just shy of 15 pounds is the Spring Lake record. The 170-acre semi-private lake has abundant stickups and minimal fishing pressure, except during the summer. Campgrounds and rental boats are available. Fortunately, concrete ramps are not unknown in this part of the state.

HOLLY AND JUNIPER SHINE

Pate speaks highly of the twosome of Holly Lake and Juniper Lake near the DeFuniak area. Both are excellent largemouth lakes with good facilities.

Juniper Lake is a flooded 'jungle' that exists just about three miles north of DeFuniak Springs. The 670-acre man made lake has yielded at least two fish over the 18 pound mark from its waters. Juniper was created in 1962 by damming a small creek. After poisoning of all fish life, restocking with sport fish began. Bass fingerlings were introduced to the waters the following spring.

In May of 1964, the impoundment was opened to the public. Clearing through the dense swamp forest was minimal, and boating over most of this 10-foot deep water is difficult. The titi trees, now dead, form an impenetrable jungle which is conducive to big bass. The holding structures are perfect largemouth lairs, and they abound in minnow and sunfish forage and protection.

The lake underwent a minor dewatering in 1974 and a major drawdown in 1984. During this time, the largemouth fed extensively on the crowded, stunted panfish population. Desirable vegetation communities were then established in areas of the lake where none previously existed. Heavy growth of coontail moss, lily pads and grass beds adds to the attraction of floating logs and submerged brush to behemoth bass. The 'unfishable' areas are undoubtedly responsible for the magnum size of largemouth in Juniper.

Evidence of the tremendous bass that Juniper yields, on occasion, exists at Clark's Landing on the lake shore. Mounted largemouth to 17 pounds hang on the walls, in addition to numerous pictures and newspaper clippings. Ten or 12 bass exceeding 12 pounds are normally taken each year from the shallow-contoured waters.

There is no charge to fish or launch a boat from the state-managed recreation area. Rental boats and campsites are available at the landing for Juniper's lunker chasers. These waters should remain very productive for many years to come, but the lunker bass angling is better in Holly Lake, according to Pate, because Juniper, being several years older, has peaked.

Located four miles north of DeFuniak Springs, Holly Lake is a private, stick-up-filled impoundment. The pay-to-fish lake was created by damming a small creek that ran through a titi swamp. Twin lakes, called in combination Lake Holly, actually were created by the earthen dam. Today, each section now has a name. The lower and larger section covering 550 acres is King Lake and the upper and smaller 250-acre section is called Holly Lake.

Only the perimeter of the original two sections were cleared for boat traffic, leaving a 'jungle' of stumps, stickups and snags over most of the lake. Stocked in 1969, Holly's spring fed waters were opened to public access in 1971. The shallow King Lake section underwent a drawdown in early 1984 to eliminate a serious

Dead Lake offers some beautiful waterways in which to cast a lure for largemouth. Many of the small, protected waters in the panhandle are conducive to angling from small craft.

vegetation problem. Approximately 80 percent of the bottom was exposed, and once refilled an average depth of seven feet was present.

The size of largemouth bass caught since has been impressive. A 16-pound, 6-ounce bass caught by Wayne Rascoe currently leads as the official lake record. Many of the giant bass in their 'teens' have been taken by wade fishermen. Bank anglers and waders were the primary users of the lake until the dam height was increased. A 128-foot fishing pier was built into the lake to allow canepole fishermen and others confined to the bank some access to deeper waters. Today, both boat anglers and bank casters catch bass.

DEER POINT LAKE

Deer Point Lake, just north of Panama City, is another panhandle impoundment worthy of note. The unique 5,000-acre reservoir was formed by constructing a dam across the upper end of North Bay. The salt water eventually turned to fresh from the headwater-spring sources of the Bear, Econfina and Cedar Creeks. The lake was then poisoned and restocked with freshwater species.

In 1964, the Panama City water supply reservoir was opened to public fishing. The lake, averaging ten feet deep, was not cleared, so some underwater structure does exist. A few road beds, deep holes of about 20 feet and stumps add to standing cypress trees along the 25-miles of shoreline which now provide bass habitat. The lake is fed by a natural freshwater stream.

Deer Point Lake had at one time a significant weed growth which deterred some anglers and frustrated others. The vegetation did, however, provide a fantastic fishery for king size largemouth. The grass carp put an end to the profuse growth and gin-clear waters, and since then, some ten pound plus bass have been caught from Deer Point. It remains a relatively productive hole to this day.

Today there is a healthy population of largemouth swimming the depths of Deer Point Lake in search of good habitat and a concentrated forage base. A handful of fish between 13 and 15 pounds have been taken in recent years, but the lake record caught in 1972 by a 12-year-old youngster stands at just over 16 pounds.

The catching on this lake is not easy, considering the clear water and dense structure. While light lines draw more strikes, the cover is an entanglement worthy of heavier monofilament. I'd suggest 12 pound test for the average weekend bass chaser. Fish the headwater creeks in the spring and fall, and check out the vegetation and stumps early and late in the day during the warmer months for best action.

Night angling is often successful here. Fish along the deeper drops off the lake's main channel. Excellent facilities exist for those interested in daylight or after dark angling for some of the lake's bass. Fish camps with rental boats and fee launching are available on the lake. Lodging is available nearby.

DAY OF THE LIVING DEAD

It is not "dead" and the watershed is more like several "lakes." Due east some 20 miles, the 25-year-old reservoir called Dead Lake lies on the Chipola River. The series of oxbow lakes and tributary creeks that existed along the river near Wewahitchka were inundated with water after construction of a dam in 1958. Thus, the unusual name exists for a single 15-mile-long body of water that covers some 9,600 acres. The dam was taken out later, but the reservoir water remains, and so does the fishing.

Dark, mirror-like waters surround cypress trees, snags, stumps, lily pads and grass beds. But the prime lunker bass habitat lies 6 to 20 feet deep in a maze of submerged timber. Some holes in the lake are 40 feet deep. Numerous fallen logs and stumps limit boat penetration deep into the 'woods' area, but big bass can be caught along the old river channel and near almost any heavy cover on this man-made lake.

Lunker largemouth to 15 pounds have been caught in the past five years. A draw-down in 1980 for weed control enhanced the lunker opportunities which average a couple dozen largemouth over ten pounds each year. The record bass from the one mile wide impoundment weighed 16 1/2 pounds. Many of Dead Lake's bass come from the tributaries.

To access the lake, drive south of Clarksville on highway 73 to the town of Wewahitchka. Cabins, motels, guides and campgrounds are available there. The Dead Lakes Recreation Area, launch ramps and other facilities for big bass chasers are also located on the lake. A special fishing permit is required of visiting anglers.

South of Dead Lake in Gulf County is Lake Wimico, a 4,055-acre natural lake accessible by boat via the Intracoastal Waterway from Apalachicola or White City. Bass are intermixed with saltwater species in this wide and shallow lake. Fishing for largemouth is fair here.

MINI-WATER DETAILS

A local permit is required on some of the waters mentioned in this chapter. Be sure to check that out. For additional information on any of the panhandle waters, contact the county chambers of commerce or the Florida Game and Fresh Water Fish Commission. They can normally provide directions and facilities locations to the better waters.

Regulations differ from one state Fish Management Area to another, so it's also wise to check with the nearest Commission Office before fishing. Other state-wide rules may vary for individual management areas. For example, cane pole anglers fishing in their own home counties are not exempt from license requirements.

Regardless of whether you fish one of the unique man made impoundments, one of the nature-carved, sand hill ponds, or a forest-hugged river, outstanding fishing for the mostly-neglected panhandle bass awaits.

16

BULLY SUNFISH SPOTS

PANHANDLE PANFISH SEEM to think they are bass when on the other end of the line. Most of our state records and some world records are held by bully fish from this region. Florida's primary shellcracker (redear sunfish) record producer, Merritt's Mill Pond in Jackson County, has yielded many whoppers. The latest, weighing 4-pounds, 13 3/4-ounces, is a world record, beating out the previous Florida and World Record by four ounces.

Marianna teenager Joey Floyd caught the 17 1/2-inch long redear sunfish on a preschool fishing trip with his father in March of 1986. The fish was almost fatter than it was long, with a girth of 16 1/2 inches. Floyd enticed the football-shaped fish to strike a cricket that he had pitched out on the bottom.

World Record warmouth bass, bluegill and redear sunfish all seem to come from panhandle ponds!

Using spinning tackle with 10-pound test Trilene line and a six-pound leader, Floyd carefully played the shellcracker before landing it. Rather than risk losing the monster, he and his father used their boat's trolling motor to follow it for seven minutes, before landing it.

The fish was the seventh state record and second world record in succession for the 202-acre, clear-water pond located two miles east of Marianna along U.S. 90. Fisheries biologists believe that the shellcrackers grow to such phenomenal size in the cypress-stained waters due to the water's purity and enormous supply of snails, a mainstay of the species' diet. Because there aren't a lot of shellcrackers in Merritt's Mill Pond, the competition for the forage is much less, resulting in some huge fish.

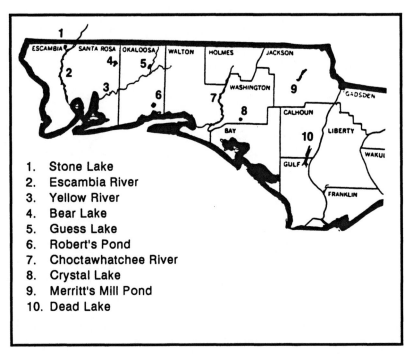

1. Stone Lake
2. Escambia River
3. Yellow River
4. Bear Lake
5. Guess Lake
6. Robert's Pond
7. Choctawhatchee River
8. Crystal Lake
9. Merritt's Mill Pond
10. Dead Lake

The redear sunfish, called shellcracker in Florida and "stumpknocker" in other parts of the South and Midwest, has a whitish-bordered gill flap that ends in a bright red spot on the male. The spot is more orange on the female. The name shellcracker is derived from the grinding teeth in the redear's throat. With them, it can crush the shell of a snail or mussel. As table fare, the pond's shellcrackers are considered excellent.

The pond is a spring-fed impoundment with waters dropping from the cypress-tree shallows to 20 feet in some places. It came into being in the 1800s and was originally called Robinson's Big Spring Creek. In 1867, a grist mill was built at the dam site, and in 1872, a man named Ethington Merritt purchased the property and the mill. It has been called Merritt's Mill Pond ever since.

Today, the sawgrass-bordered waters are backed up by a dam built by the Florida public utilities. There is plenty of fishing pressure on the pond, and the clear water can make angling difficult. The 4 1/2-mile-long state management water has a "giant shellcracker" reputation, but don't overlook the bluegill and bass fishing here. It still produces many respectable largemouth. Some over 10 pounds have been taken.

The small waters of the panhandle produce some fish which only think they are bass, like this world record redear sunfish (shellcracker). It was caught in Merritt's Mill Pond.

The best fishing on the mill pond is usually in the early spring, late March or early April. The fish go on their beds early here as the clear water begins to quickly warm after the winter chill. Since the spring's 123 million gallons a day influx replaces the pond's total volume so rapidly, the water temperature changes only slightly in the winter months. For this reason, the big shellcrackers spawn about six weeks ahead of the fish in other area waters.

Boiling though a limestone layer, the spring water is quite "hard." The mineral-rich water is also clean and pure. The average year around temperature is about 72 degrees.

TODAY'S TACTICS AND THE FUTURE

Thin line in small test is best for this fishing. An ultra-light spinning rod and reel spooled with 4 pound test clear monofilament to usually employed by area experts. Use a No. 6 or No. 8 hook for the small-mouthed fish. Red wigglers, earthworms and crickets weighted down by a single splitshot, jigs, flies or small artificials will fool their share.

Drift fishing along the edges of the open spring run is often most productive. Minimize use of the trolling motor and paddle in

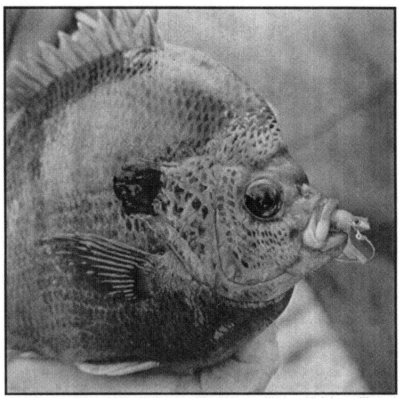

Big redear sunfish and bluegill (bream) like this one will hit artificials readily and quite likely, surprise some largemouth bass anglers.

the super-clear water. Cloudy and rainy days and moonlit nights offer the best chances to catch a giant shellcracker or largemouth.

Despite the unique shellcracker fishing, state fisheries biologists have noticed an alarming decline of aquatic plants and sport fish populations in the pond. Twenty years ago, the vegetation covered almost all of the pond. Much less cover was available prior to its 12-foot drawdown and restoration in 1990. Layers of muck which had accumulated on the pond's bottom were exposed to sunlight and air.

The mill pond has been drawn down three times for various reasons since 1956. However, those short-term drawdowns resulted in very little or no drying and compaction of the pond's bottom. The shellcrackers which appear to be genetically superior to others in the state were collected and placed in a hatchery during the latest drawdown. They were allowed to spawn in the hatchery ponds and were, along with their offspring, restocked into the pond following the drawdown.

Fantastic fishing could result in the next two years, according to the biologists involved in the restoration. The Florida Public Utilities Company has the responsibility of regulating water levels on the pond. There is one public boat ramp on the pond that varies in width from 100 to 300 yards, and an RV and tent campground located at the site of the old grist mill.

RECORD BLUEGILL

A bluegill which though it was a big largemouth was caught by a Chipley man. The Florida record came from Crystal Lake in Washington County. It weighed 2 pounds, 15 1/4 ounces and measured 13 3/4 inches in total length. The fish, with a girth of 15 1/4 inches, was shaped like a basketball!

John LeMaster fooled the trophy-sized panfish at night. He was slow-trolling a live cricket through deep waters. The bait was attached to 6-pound test line and was weighted down only by a barrel swivel. One doesn't need heavy-duty or fancy equipment to take these fish.

North Florida waters typically give up the state's largest bluegill. The previous record was taken in 1985 from a pond in Columbia County and weighed just over one ounce less than LeMaster's 'gill. It was caught on a cane pole by a 3-year old boy who was fishing with his grandfather. That pond had been stocked with 1-inch long bluegills just 7 years earlier.

WARMOUTH "BASS" COUNTRY

World records come in all sizes, depending on the species. One of the smallest "giants" is a warmouth bass caught in October of 1985 in Okaloosa County, Florida. The 2-pound, 7-ounce fish was almost 40 percent heavier than the previous Florida state record and bested the world record Fresh Water Fishing Hall of Fame mark by five ounces.

Tony Dempsey landed the huge warmouth from Guess Lake, a tiny, natural slough off the Yellow River. The 22-year old used 12-pound test line on spinning tackle and nightcrawlers for bait to entice the 13 1/2 inch long specimen. The fish that fought like a bass measured 13 1/4 inches in girth.

The Crestview angler battled the warmouth for five minutes before bringing it to the bank. Dempsey then contacted a local wildlife officer who verified weight and species. The Yellow River is not the only panhandle water with king-size warmouth. The Choctawhatchee River is the top producer in Walton, Holmes, and Washington counties. Robert's Pond on the Eglin Air Force Base in Okaloosa County is where the previous state warmouth mark was caught, and it remains a productive spot. In Escambia and Santa Rosa counties, the Escambia River is usually hard to beat for action and Dead Lake in Gulf County has some whopper warmouth also. Stone Lake in Escambia County and Bear Lake in the Blackwater State Forest (Santa Rosa County) are great panfish spots managed by the Commission. Contact their Panama City office for more information.

APPENDICES

Appendix A - County by County Lakes and Acreage

Appendix B - Contact Information and Chambers of Commerce

Appendix C - Fishing & Hunting Resource Directory

Appendix D - Fishing Hot Spots Maps

Index

APPENDIX A

NORTH FLORIDA WATER BODIES & ACREAGE

Alachua County
Lake Alto 540
Holdens Pond 80
Johnson Lake 52
Little Orange Lake 818
Little Santa Fe Lake 1,135
Lake Lochloosa 5,705
Newnans Lake 7,427
Orange Lake 12,706
Santa Fe Lake 4,721
Watermelon Pond 531
Lake Wauberg 248

Baker County
Osceola Ponds (3) 21

Bay County
Deer Point Lake 5,000
Econfina Creek 60
Martin Bayou 240

Bradford County
Crosby Lake 558
Hampton lake 823
Rowell Lake 364
Sampson Lake 2,042

Calhoun County
Lake Hilda 10

Clay County
Blue Pond 202
Brooklyn Lake 645
Doctors Lake 3,397
Geneva Lake 1,630
Johnson Lake 480
Kingsley Lake 1,652
Lowery Lake 1,263
Magnolia Lake 205

Columbia County
Alligator Lake 338
Ichetucknee River 100
Lake Jeffery 114
Montgomery Lake 36
Ocean Pond 1,774
Santa Fe River 5,000
Watertown Lake 46

Dixie County
Suwannee River 12,000

Duval County
Black Creek 450
Cedar River 150
Hanna Park Pond 40
Julington Creek 900
Ortega River 675
Ribault River 150

Escambia County
Perdido River 800
Stone Lake 130

Franklin County
Apalachicola River 30,000
Crooked River 900

Gadsden County
Lake Talquin 8,850

Gilchrist County
Waters Lake 166

Gulf County
Dead Lakes 3,655
Lake Wimico 4,055

Hamilton County
Withlacoochee River 647

Holmes County
Lake Victor 130

Jackson County
Chipola River 290
Compass Lake 581
Merritt's Mill Pond 202
Ocheesee Pond 2,225
Round Lake 33
Lake Seminole (Fl) 3,200

Jefferson County
Aucilla River 250
Lake Miccosukee 6,276
Snead's Smokehouse 81
Wacissa River 250

Lafayette County
Lake Townsend 110

Leon County
Carr Lake 400
Lake Hall 172
Lake Iamonia 5,757
Lake Jackson 4,000
Lake Munson 255

Levy County
Waccasassa River 210

Madison County
Cherry Lake 479
Lake Francis 21
Mystic Lake 47

Nassau County
Boggy Creek 360
Lofton Creek 300
Mills Creek 100
Nassau River 5,000
Plummers Lake 75
St. Mary's River 3,651
Thomas Creek 50

Okaloosa County
Karick Lake 58
Shoal River 42
Hurricane Lake 350

Santa Rosa County
Bear Lake 107
Blackwater River 700
Escambia River 500
Yellow River 700

St. Johns County
St. Johns River 96,000
Guano Lake 1,800

Suwannee County
Peacock Lake 148
Suwannee Lake 63

Taylor County
Econfina River 270
Fenholloway River 175
Steinhatchee River 150

Union County
Lake Butler 420
New River 150
Palestine Lake 911
Swift Creek 568

Wakulla County
Lake Ellen 150
Ochlockonee River 750
Otter Lake 133
Sopchoppy River 150
St. Marks River 140
Wakulla River 248

Walton County
Choctawhatchee River 280
Jackson Lake 210
Juniper Lake 670
Kings Lake 300
Lake Stanley 100
Western Lake 220

Washington County
Gap Pond 527
Holmes Creek 134
Pate Lake 1,045
Smith Lake 160

APPENDIX B

NORTH FLORIDA COUNTY CHAMBERS OF COMMERCE

Alachua County
P.O. Box 387
Alachua, FL 32615
904/462-3333

Baker County
20 East Macclenny Ave.
Macclenny, FL 32063
904/259-6433

Bay County
P.O. Box 1850
Panama City, FL 32402
904/785-5206

Bradford County
P.O. Box 576
Starke, FL 32091
904/964-5278

Calhoun County
314 E. Central Ave.
Blountstown, FL 32424
904/674-4519

Clay County
P.O. Box 1441
Orange Park, FL 32067
904/264-2651

Columbia County
P.O.Box 566
Lake City, FL 32056
904/752-3690

Dixie County
P.O. Box 547
Cross City, FL 32628
904/498-3367

Duval County/Jacksonville
P.O. Box 329
Jacksonville, FL 32201
904/353-0300

Escambia County/Pensacola Area
P.O. Box 550
Pensacola, FL 32593
904/438-4081

Franklin County/Apalachicola Bay
128 Market St.
Apalachicola, FL 32320
904/653-9419

Gadsden
P.O. Box 389
Quincy, FL 32351
904/627-9231

Gilchrist County
P.O. Box 186
Trenton, FL 32693
904/463-6327

Gulf County
P.O. Box 628
Wewahitchka, FL 32465
904/639-2130

Hamilton County
P.O. Drawer P
Jasper, FL 32052
904/792-1300

Holmes County
P.O. Box 1977
Bonifay, FL 32425
904/547-4682

Jackson County
P.O. Box 130
Marianna, FL 32446
904/482-8061

Jefferson County/Monticello
420 West Washington Ave.
Monticello, FL 32344
904/997-5552

173

Lafayette County
P.O. Box 416
Mayo, FL 32066
904/294-2918

Leon County/Tallahassee
P.O. Box 1639
Tallahassee, FL 32302
904/224-8116

Levy County/Chiefland Area
P.O. Box 1397
Chiefland, FL 32626
904/726-2801

Madison County
105 North Range St.
Madison, FL 32340
904/973-2788

Nassau County/Amelia Island
P.O. Box 472
Fernandina Beach, FL 32034
904/261-3248

Okaloosa County/Crestview
502 S. Main Street
Crestview, FL 32536
904/682-3212

Santa Rosa County
501 Milton Street SW
Milton, FL 32570
904/623-2339

St. Johns County
P.O. Drawer O
St. Augustine, FL 32085
904/829-5681

Suwannee County
P.O. Drawer C
Live Oak, FL 32060
904/362-3071

Taylor County
P.O. Box 892
Perry, FL 32347
904/584-0888

Union County
P.O. Box 797
Lake Butler, FL 32054
904/496-3624

Wakulla County
P.O. Box 598
Crawfordville, FL 32327
904/926-1848

Walton County
P.O. Box 29
DeFuniak Springs, FL 32433
904/892-3191

Washington County
P.O. Box 457
Chipley, FL 32428
904/638-4157

OTHER CONTACTS

Florida Game and Fresh Water
Fish Commission
620 S. Meridian St.,
Tallahassee, FL 32399

Jim Woodruff Dam, Lake
Seminole, U.S. Army Corps of
Engineers, P.O. Box 96,
Chattahoochee, FL 32324;
(912)662-2001

Florida Dept. of Natural
Resources
3900 Commonwealth Blvd.
Tallahassee, FL 32399

Georgia Dept. of Natural
Resources
270 Washington St. SW
Atlanta, GA 30334

Apalachicola National Estuarine Reserve (904) 653-8063

FISHING & HUNTING RESOURCE DIRECTORY

If you are interested in more productive fishing and hunting trips, then this info is for you!

Larsen's Outdoor Publishing is the publisher of several quality Outdoor Libraries - all informational-type books that focus on how and where to catch America's most popular sport fish, hunt America's most popular big game or travel to productive or exciting destinations.

The perfect-bound, soft-cover books include numerous illustrative  graphics, line drawings, maps and photographs. The BASS SERIES LIBRARY and the two HUNTING LIBRARIES are nationwide in scope. The INSHORE SERIES covers coastal areas from Texas to Maryland and foreign waters. The OUTDOOR TRAVEL SERIES covers the most popular fishing and diving destinations in the world. The BASS WATERS SERIES focuses on the top lakes and rivers in the nation's most visited largemouth bass fishing state.

All series appeal to outdoorsmen/readers of all skill levels. The unique four-color cover design, interior layout, quality, information content and economical price makes these books hot sellers in the marketplace. Best of all, you can learn to be more successful in your outdoor endeavors!!

175

THE BASS SERIES LIBRARY
by Larry Larsen

1. FOLLOW THE FORAGE FOR BETTER BASS ANGLING VOL. 1 BASS/PREY RELATIONSHIP
Learn how to determine the dominant forage in a body of water, and you will consistently catch more and larger bass. Whether you fish artificial lures or live bait, your bass stringer will benefit!

2. FOLLOW THE FORAGE FOR BETTER BASS ANGLING VOL. 2 TECHNIQUES
Learn why one lure or bait is more successful than others and how to use each lure under varying conditions. You will also learn highly productive patterns that will catch bass under most circumstances!

3. BASS PRO STRATEGIES
Professional fishermen know how changes in pH, water temperature, color and fluctuations affect bass fishing, and they know how to adapt to weather and topographical variations. Learn from their experience. Your productivity will improve after spending a few hours with this compilation of tactics!

4. BASS LURES - TRICKS & TECHNIQUES
When bass become accustomed to the same artificials and presentations seen over and over again, they become harder to catch. Learn how to rig or modify your lures and develop specific presentation and retrieve methods to spark or renew the interest of largemouth!

5. SHALLOW WATER BASS
Bass spend 90% of their time in the shallows, and you spend the majority of the time fishing for them in waters less than 15 feet deep. Learn specific productive tactics that you can apply to fishing in marshes, estuaries, reservoirs, lakes, creeks and small ponds. You'll likely triple your results!

THE BASS SERIES LIBRARY
by Larry Larsen

6. BASS FISHING FACTS

Learn why and how bass behave during pre- and post-spawn, how they utilize their senses and how they respond to their environment, and you'll increase your bass angling success! This angler's guide to the lifestyles and behavior of the black bass is a reference source never before compiled. It examines how bass utilize their senses to feed. By applying this knowledge, your productivity will increase for largemouth as well as Redeye, Suwannee, Spotted and other bass species.

7. TROPHY BASS

If you're more interested in wrestling with one or two monster largemouth than with a "panfull" of yearlings, then learn what techniques and habitats will improve your chances. This book takes a look at geographical areas and waters that offer better opportunities to catch giant bass, as well as proven methods and tactics for both man made and natural waters. The "how to" information was gleaned from professional guides and other experienced trophy bass hunters.

8. ANGLER'S GUIDE TO BASS PATTERNS

Catch bass every time out by learning how to develop a productive pattern quickly and effectively. Learn the most effective combination of lures, methods and places. Understanding bass movement and activity and the most appropriate and effective techniques to employ will add many pounds of enjoyment to the sport of bass fishing.

9. BASS GUIDE TIPS

Learn the most productive methods of top bass fishing guides in the country and secret techniques known only in a certain region or state that may work in your waters. Special features include shiners, sunfish kites & flies; flippin, pitchin' & dead stickin' rattlin; skippin' & jerk baits; moving, deep, hot & cold waters; fronts, high winds & rain. New approaches for bass angling success!

INSHORE SERIES
by Frank Sargeant

IL1. THE SNOOK BOOK
"Must" reading for anyone who loves the pursuit of this unique sub-tropic species. Every aspect of how you can find and catch big snook is covered, in all seasons and all waters where snook are found.

IL2. THE REDFISH BOOK
Packed with expertise from the nation's leading redfish anglers and guides, this book covers every aspect of finding and fooling giant reds. You'll learn secret techniques revealed for the first time.

IL3. THE TARPON BOOK
Find and catch the wily "silver king" along the Gulf Coast, north through the mid-Atlantic, and south along Central and South American coastlines. Numerous experts share their most productive techniques.

IL4. THE TROUT BOOK - *COMING SOON!*
You'll learn the best seasons, techniques and lures in this comprehensive book.

OUTDOOR TRAVEL SERIES
by Timothy O'Keefe and Larry Larsen

A candid guide with inside information on the best charters, time of the year, and other vital recommendations that can make your next fishing and/or diving trip much more enjoyable.

OT1. FISH & DIVE THE CARIBBEAN - Volume 1
Northern Caribbean, including Cozumel, Caymans Bahamas, Virgin Islands and other popular destinations.

OT2. FISH & DIVE THE CARIBBEAN - Volume 2 - *COMING SOON!* Southern Caribbean, including Guadeloupe, Bonaire, Costa Rica, Venezuela and other destinations.

DEER HUNTING LIBRARY
by John E. Phillips

DH1. MASTERS' SECRETS OF DEER HUNTING
Increase your deer hunting success significantly by learning from the masters of the sport. New information on tactics and strategies for bagging deer is included in this book, the most comprehensive of its kind.

DH2. THE SCIENCE OF DEER HUNTING - *COMING SOON!*

TURKEY HUNTING LIBRARY
by John E. Phillips

TH1. MASTERS' SECRETS OF TURKEY HUNTING
Masters of the sport have solved some of the most difficult problems you will encounter while hunting wily longbeards with bows, blackpowder guns and shotguns. Learn 10 deadly sins of turkey hunting and what to do if you commit them.

TH2. OUTSMART TOUGH TURKEYS - *COMING SOON!*

BASS WATERS SERIES
by Larry Larsen
Take the guessing game out of your next bass fishing trip. The most productive bass waters in each region of the state are described in this multi-volume series, including boat ramp information, seasonal tactics, water characteristics and much more. Popular and overlooked lakes, rivers, streams, ponds, canals, marshes and estuaries are clearly detailed with numerous maps and drawings.

BW1. GUIDE TO NORTH FLORIDA BASS WATERS
From Orange Lake north and west.

BW2. GUIDE TO CENTRAL FLORIDA BASS WATERS
From Tampa/Orlando to Palatka.

BW3. GUIDE TO SOUTH FLORIDA BASS WATERS
COMING SOON! - from I-4 to the Everglades.

INDEX

182